"not my way" 86
Hardy, 89-90   Some
                      Underlining
Mottram, 93   5 —
anti-Auden, 97   HD
Carruth, 114
Kinnell/life poetry, 150
"poetry in the act of
        writing poetry," 159
"to be good, try to be great," 172

Goatfoot
Milktongue
Twinbird

Poets on Poetry

Donald Hall, General Editor

Goatfoot Milktongue Twinbird

Interviews, Essays, and Notes on Poetry, 1970-76

DONALD HALL

Ann Arbor   The University of Michigan Press

Library of Congress Cataloging in Publication Data

Hall, Donald, 1928-
Goatfoot milktongue twinbird.

(Poets on poetry)
1. Hall, Donald, 1928-   —Interviews.
2. Poetry—Collected works.   3. Poets, American—
20th century—Interviews.   I. Title.   II. Series.
PS3515.A3152Z52 1977   811'.5'4   77-3248
ISBN 0-472-40000-2

Acknowledgments

Grateful acknowledgment is made to the following journals and publishers for permission to reprint copyrighted material:

Agenda Editions, 5 Cranbourne Court, Albert Bridge Road, London, England, for material from *Agenda*, "Questions from *Agenda*."

American Poetry Review, 401 South Broad Street, Philadelphia, Pennsylvania, for numerous extracted "Knock Knock" columns written over the years by Donald Hall.

Best Cellar Press, 118 South Boswell, Crete, Nebraska, for material from *Pebble*, "Some Ideas about Prose Poems."

British Broadcasting Corporation, 630 Fifth Avenue, New York, New York, and Manchester, England, for "Larkin and Larkinism" which originated as a BBC broadcast.

Brockport Writers Forum for "An Interview: With Gregory Fitz Gerald and Rodney Parshall," edited from a prose transcription of a videotape interview with Donald Hall in April, 1972, sponsored by the Brockport Writers Forum, Department of English, State University College, Brockport, N.Y. 14420. All rights reserved, State University of New York.

David McKay Company, 750 Third Avenue, New York, New York, for "More Questions." First appeared in *The Creative Process*, edited by Alberta T. Turner. Copyright © 1977 by David McKay Company, Inc. Reprinted by permission of the publisher.

Field: Contemporary Poetry and Poetics, Rice Hall, Oberlin College, Oberlin, Ohio, for "The Line," *Field*, no. 10, and "Goatfoot, Milktongue, Twinbird: The Psychic Origins of Poetic Form," *Field*, no. 9.

Nation, 333 Sixth Avenue, New York, New York, for "Geoffrey Hill's Poems," *Nation*, December 6, 1975, and "Kinnell: A Luminous Receptiveness," *Nation*, October 11, 1971.

New York Times Company, 229 West 43rd Street, New York, New York, for "Last Word" ("Shakespeare's Lines in Academic Dress") by Donald Hall, *New York Times Book Review*, March 14, 1976. Copyright © 1976 by the New York Times Company. Reprinted by permission.

Ohio Review, 346 Ellis Hall, Ohio University, Athens, Ohio, for "Trapping Pterodactyls: An Interview with Donald Hall" ("An Interview: With Wayne Dodd and Stanley Plumly"), *Ohio Review* 15, no. 3 (Spring 1974), copyright © 1974 by Ohio University; and "Notes on Robert Bly and *Sleepers Joining Hands*."

St. Martin's Press, Inc., and St. James Press Ltd., for "Robert Lowell" from *Contemporary Poets* by R. Murphy.

Spoken Arts, Inc., 310 North Avenue, New Rochelle, New York, for "Poems Aloud," liner notes from *The Pleasures of Poetry*.

The Review, 11 Greek Street, London, England, for material used in "Questions from *The Review*."

Trellis, PO Box 656, Morgantown, West Virginia, for "Words Without Bodies," *First Trellis Supplement*.

Every effort has been made to trace the ownership of all copyrighted material in this book and to obtain permission for its use.

For Frances McCullough

Preface

After the thirties and forties, when American poets lost themselves in their own New Criticism, younger poets reacted by putting literary criticism on the poetic index. Or so it has seemed. In fact, poets kept on talking about poetry, and criticizing each others' work, but they used forms more tentative than full-dress essays published in literary quarterlies. The interview printed as dialog, initiated by the *Paris Review*, became the dominant form by which poets made public their poetics. For more practical purposes, like defining or urging taste, there was still the book review; some even tried their hands at an essay from time to time, while looking the other way. But for many years, poets did not collect their criticism into books.

Recently, poets have begun to come out of their critical closets. Robert Creeley's essays and interviews have been collected. W. D. Snodgrass assembled his lectures and essays as *In Radical Pursuit*. Allen Ginsberg published a book of interviews. Louis Simpson wrote a critical book about Pound, Eliot, and Williams.

In this collection, I merely assemble my periodical talk about poetry from the last several years. Still, I would hope this book might be useful to young poets trying out their ideas. Most likely to sharpen their claws on.

The first note collected here was written in 1968, and began a direction I continued later; everything else comes from the seventies. This concentration in time may lend the collection unity, but of course unity can be another word for repetitiousness. I am aware that some of my notions begin in one interview, get rephrased in another, take on essay form a few pages later, and later still undergo qualification. (I am obsessed; you repeat yourself; he has only one thing to say.) I hope that these threads may interweave with more decoration than redundancy.

Occasions for these notes were various—reviews, questionnaires, interviews, a regular column in the *American Poetry Review*, a BBC talk—and different occasions sponsor different tones of voice: the interviewer is obviously a collaborator; "The Vatic Voice" was addressed to psychologists; "Larkin and Larkinism" was written to outrage an English radio audience.

I have made a few stylistic changes when I was uncomfortable with the earlier phrasing. I would like to have made more, but it seemed like cheating. I have not changed ideas or opinions, but I have removed one or two. In the interviews the interviewer's questions are in italic type and my responses are in roman type. I have also removed references to forthcoming books which forthcame some years ago. The order of this book is chronological, by date of composition, from 1968 through 1975.

D. H.

Wilmot, N. H.

June, 1976

Contents

The Vatic Voice

Today, I want to talk about the first moment of the creative process—the excited flash of insight, coming in the shape of images, a rush of words before which one often feels like a passive observer—rather than talk about elaboration—getting the words right, learning how to cross out the wrong words, learning how to stimulate the secondary inspiration of revision. I am talking in terms of poetry, but I think my terms apply to other endeavors also.

A premise: within every human being there is the vatic voice. *Vates* was the Greek word for the inspired bard, speaking the words of a god. To most people, this voice speaks only in dream, and only in unremembered dream. The voice may shout messages into the sleeping ear, but a guard at the horned gate prevents the waking mind from remembering, listening, interpreting. It is the vatic voice (which is not necessarily able to write good poetry, or even passable grammar) which rushes forth the words of excited recognition, which supplies what we call inspiration. And inspiration,

---

This note was first prepared for delivery at the National Council of Teachers of English Conference on Creativity, at Colorado Springs in November of 1968.

a breathing-into, is a perfectly expressive metaphor: "Not I, not I, but the wind that blows through me!" as Lawrence says. Or Shelley's "Ode to the West Wind." We are passive to the vatic voice, as the cloud or the tree is passive to the wind.

Just this month I have had an odd experience with a student who is trying to write poems. I let him into the writing class liking part of his examples, but not convinced of his talent. The first poems he showed me were wordy, explanatory, sincere, and dull. Then I happened to tell the whole class an anecdote about Hart Crane, who sometimes stimulated first-drafts by listening to Ravel, very loud, and about Gertrude Stein, who wrote while parked at Parisian intersections with all the horns beeping. They were using sound to clear away the tops of their minds. A week later my student came to office hours excited. He had been trying something. He had been listening to music, earphones clapped to his head and volume turned way up, and writing, "Whatever came into my head." He had a series of small fragments of astonishingly new and original imagery. The lines weren't finished, the rhythm wasn't very good, here and there was a cliché or a dead metaphor. But there was astonishing originality in each poem; some corner of new light, and what I can only call an extraordinary original intelligence. I think that in his case the apparatus of the ordinary intelligence had conspired to make his old poems pedestrian. When he was able to remove the top of his mind by this external stimulus of noise, the vatic voice broke through. He still has a way to go to learn to make his imaginings into good poems, but that is another matter.

I make up the phrase, "the vatic voice," not because I am especially in love with it—it sounds pretentious—but because I am trying to avoid using words that have acquired either more precise meanings, or more precise affectations of meaning, like "the unconscious mind." Anyway, the unconscious mind does not talk directly to us.

Two characteristics that distinguish the vatic voice from normal discourse are that it is always original, and that we feel passive to it. We are surprised by it, and we may very well, having uttered its words, not know what we mean.

We must find ways to let this voice speak. We want to get loose, we want to regress in the service of the ego, we want to become as children. We want to do this not only to make poems, or to invent a new theory of linguistics, but because it feels good, because it is healthy and therapeutic, because it helps us to understand ourselves, and to be able to love other people. I think, I truly think, that to clear the passageway to the insides of ourselves, to allow the vatic voice to speak through us, is the *ultimate* goal to which men must address themselves. It is what to live for, it is what to live by.

Poetry is evidence of the vatic speech, but it is also typically an exhortation toward the vatic condition. Never to hear this voice in remembered night dream, or in day dream, or in moments of transport, is to be a lamentable figure, a lamentable figure frequent on college campuses. Children all hear it. This is a romantic cliché, and it is an observable truth. "There is another world that lives in the air." Most bad poetry—that which is not mere technical incompetence, technical competence can be acquired—is a result of defective creative process, which is a result of neurosis. That is, bad poetry is largely the result of being a lamentable man.

Sometimes I have tried to keep in touch with this vatic voice by sleeping a lot. Taking short naps can be a great means of keeping the channel open. There is that wonderful long, delicious slide or drift down heavy air to the bottom of sleep, which you touch for only a moment, and then there is the floating up again, more swiftly, through an incredible world of images, sometimes in bright colors. I come out of these fifteen or twenty minute naps, not with phrases of poetry, but wholly refreshed, with the experience of losing control and entering a world of total freedom. I wake with great energy. On occasion, I remember phrases or scenes from dreams, either night dreams, or nap dreams, or waking fantasy dreams—and take these phrases or images directly into a poem. That happens, but it is not the only virtue of dream. Dream is the spirit dying into the underworld, and being born again.

There is also the deliberate farming of daydream. There is a way in which you can daydream quite loosely, but also observe yourself. You watch the strange associations, the movements. These associations are frequently trying to tell us something. The association is always there for some reason. Listen. When you hum a tune, remember the words that go with the tune and you will usually hear some part of your mind commenting on another part of your mind, or on some recent action.

There is something I want to call peripheral vision, and I don't mean anything optical. If you talk about a dream with an analyst, and there is an old battered table in the dream that you casually mention, he may well say, "What about this table? What did it look like?" Often these little details are so important. When I am listening to something passively speaking out to me, I don't attempt to choose what is most important, I try to listen to all of it. I never know what is going to be the most important message until I have lived with it for a while. Very frequently, the real subject matter is something only glimpsed, as if it were out of the corner of the eye. Often the association which at first glance appears crazy and irrelevant ultimately leads to the understanding, and tells what we did not know before. I don't know how to stimulate peripheral vision. But one can train the mind to observe the periphery rather than to ignore it. Remember: if you are thinking about something, and you have one really crazy, totally irrelevant, nutty, useless, unimaginably silly association, listen hard; it's the whole point, almost without a doubt.

Mostly, when the vatic voice speaks through me, I have not stimulated its appearance in any way. I do not know how to make it happen. I know that it comes frequently when I have been busy on other materials. The way I am living now, poetry, and new ideas in general, are apt to come out of a busy schedule, as a kind of alternative to, relief from, or even infidelity to more conventional duties. But I do not mean to generalize; this will not be true of all people, or even true of me six months from now.

I do know that as you grow older you can learn better how to listen to this voice inside yourself. You can learn better not to dismiss it, you can learn not to be frightened of it. You can learn to stay loose enough to let it keep talking and yet attentive enough to remember and record it. When the voice is silent one can only wait. One can only try to keep the channels open, to stay ready for the voice, which will come when it chooses to come. Staying ready for the voice involves not being frightened, hung up, tight, mature, intellectual, reasonable, or otherwise neurotic.

An Interview
With Scott Chisholm

Mr. Hall, you were born and raised in New England. Would you comment on early influences which led you to write in the first place?

It's always a series of trivialities and accidents. I grew up in the suburbs of New Haven, Connecticut—a town called Hamden. I spent all my summers on a farm in New Hampshire where my mother's father and mother lived. They were one-horse farmers. It was not economical to run small farms any more. My grandmother is still there, at ninety-two. It's the house she was born in. That is the place where I kept to myself and day-dreamed. From twelve on, I wrote poems there. I loved my grandfather very much. We'd be in the tie-up and he'd be milking and he would recite poems to entertain me. They weren't good poems; they were pieces he used to recite at the Lyceum when he was a young man. He was a great piece-speaker—very dramatic, great gestures.

When I was about twelve, and in seventh grade, I got interested in *being* something romantic and appealing. (You can begin any art for a silly reason, and then the art itself can take hold of you.) I was a lousy athlete, and I wanted some alternative way to get attention, especially from girls. Cheerleaders. I was interested in acting and writing. I wrote my first poem then. I wrote a few more, and I tried to write some fiction. Then, when I was fourteen, I became enormously excited about poetry. The friends that I gradually made at high school mostly had some interest in the arts. The girls I dated were going to be actresses; one boy wanted to become a composer. We were the oddballs in high school; but even being strange—that sense of alienation—was something I wanted and liked and fed upon. So I kept on writing poems. I used to come home from school, frequently after rehearsing a play, and work on poems for a couple of hours. One thing that strikes me as strange is that, right away, I began revising poems. I would finish a poem, and then I would start it over again, making changes. As far as my parents were concerned, I was to do what I liked. When I was sixteen, they sent me to Bread Loaf Writers' Conference, where I met Robert Frost.

I got excited about being a poet at fourteen, and I just kept on. My girl friends who were going to be actresses stopped. I don't think I had any more talent at fourteen than anybody else did. I just kept on. I wanted to, so much. Really, I never hesitated; there was never any dramatic point in my life where I made a decision or looked back and saw that I had made a decision.

I suppose that a person could say that a great deal of your work involves the sense of loss. In your prose pieces, especially in String Too Short to Be Saved, *there is the sense of lost people, places, events—and a good deal about your grandfather. Those characteristics carry over to your poetry in poems like "Old Home Day." Are you aware of the sense of loss as a motivating factor in your work?*

I'm aware when I read it, I'm not aware of it as a motivation to become a poet, for instance. Of course, a tremendous amount of poetry is elegiac—not just over death, but over the loss of youth, or the loss of friends.

I used to think that this was a temperamental thing with me. I used to think that it was connected with New Hampshire, a disappearing country, a place where, every year, there were more farms abandoned, and where, when you walked through the woods in the pasture-land, you had to watch where you put your feet for fear you might fall into a well or an old cellar hole. I used to think that this was my conditioning. But now I think my conditioning must have been earlier, and that's one reason why I liked New Hampshire, because it fulfilled the sense of loss I already had. I've come to think that the sense of being abandoned is central to my spirit. Sometimes I think we might get this from the memory of being born. Being born is a kind of abandonment and loss—loss of that comfort of the fluid and warmth inside the womb, out into the hostile air that makes you cry. I don't know. I can only talk out of my feelings and make guesses. Certainly, it could go back to wailing in your crib when your mother has gone next door to talk to a neighbor, or when someone who is supposed to look after you forgets you for a while. The sense of loss or abandonment wells up strong in your life when something in the present touches down on that old feeling.

I think that poems happen mostly when something in the present—something that you observe, something that moves you—reaches back into something very deep and probably very old in your head. It's like when two pieces of the mineral get together in an arc light: a spark jumps across it. Poetry happens in this near-collision of the two things; the words start coming, the images start forming.

And so the poem, insofar as a poem is about anything, is about these two distinct events. This accounts for the fact that poems are written in layers—a top side of the poem that the poet and his audience may be immediately aware of, and an underside of the poem which the poet is not aware of at the point of composition, which he may never be aware of, and which the audience in reading may not be aware of—but which, in fact, moves the poet to write and moves the reader to respond. This communication is not intellectual. It is the communication of one inside speaking to another inside.

You didn't always talk the same way about poetry, did you? At Oxford, for example, you once said, "The best poems are utterly controlled and formal," and on another occasion you wrote that, "All doctrines of inspiration have been invented by amateurs and poseurs." Do you still hold to these attitudes—or have you modified them? (laughter)

I haven't modified them; I've just reversed them.

That statement was partly a reaction to Englishmen talking about inspiration in a wispy way which simply meant that they wouldn't take poetry seriously. But it's only partly that. What I hear mostly in those sentences is a shriek of terror—a fear of inspiration, a fear of the imagination, a fear of the loss of control.

Earlier, you asked me about the influence of New England. Now, I don't know if this is the influence of New England or not (it sounds as if it could be) but I certainly grew up with two opposite things in my head concerning poetry. One was that I loved it; I loved the form of it, the feel of it, the beauty of it. A good poem has a sensual body: they're lovely and beautiful, like women, like sculpture.

On the other side—the second side—there was a part of me that really knew that poetry was wicked. Poetry was associated with things like opium dens, the white slave trade. I mean, it was a wicked thing to do. Like women! [laughter] The proper thing to do, I suppose, was to be the business man—putting in his hours of work for his family. Poetry was an exotic thing. It was like being captain of a pirate ship or something. I use these childish descriptions because I think it was like that.

I wanted it both ways. You try to satisfy both sides of your ambivalence. And so I made poems that were controlled by technique and reason.

I asserted control because the real freedom of poetry, the loosening of the impulse of unconscious things that are primitive and conventionally reprehensible—that loosening frightened me. A lot of New England, a lot of Harvard, and a lot of Oxford went along with this fear about poetry. I wrote poetry that was antipoetic. Eventually, in my life, I got over much of this fear, so that I could love the sensual body of the poem and try to make poems which are, in themselves as objects, beautiful. But I used to be frightened of what the content might reveal to other people. I think that in the concentration on technique, on control, in the denial of inspiration, you hear a man saying, "Please. I don't want to hear anything inside myself that isn't upright, moral, true, loyal"—the whole Boy Scout Oath.

Speaking of technique, you once wrote that "All American writers, in one way or another, are obsessed with their technique." Do you feel that this is an obsession which opposes certain freedoms or innovations in poetry?

I think it's a device by which we often keep ourselves from innovation. But it goes both ways, as I say about everything. Whenever I make a spiritual innovation in poetry, for myself, something happens which is technically different. The poem makes a different noise. Years ago, it seemed to me that by experimenting with the technical side of poetry, I allowed voices to speak out of me that hadn't been able to speak before. Now I'm suspicious of the order of events. Perhaps, the first thing was really the voice wanting to speak. Perhaps the voice was really running me and disguising itself as a search for new technique, in order to let me ride it, in order to let it come out. I talk as if I'm running a boardinghouse inside myself.

If concentration on technique allows poets to grow, it's fine. Many people, however, get stuck in technique and don't go any further. This was especially true for many of us who were beginning to write poetry after the Second World War. The concentration on technique can become infantile. You can get stuck in the "playing" aspect of words. I do not regret, at the moment, that I spent so much time thinking about line breaks, and vowels, because I think that in the preconscious—not the unconscious but the preconscious—I gathered a lot of knowledge. It's like an athlete, practicing a lot, who learns to make moves which, in a particular game, he does without thinking. He moves as if by instinct—but it's not instinct: it's something learned which resides in you without you thinking about it.

Obviously, you learn tremendously from reading the poets and loving them. This knowledge enters your preconscious and forms your idea of what the sensual body of a poem may be. But you also learn by your own writing and devising. When I write poems now, I never think about wit or technique—about showing off and playing with words. I revise what doesn't sound right to something that sounds better. I think the sounding-not-so-right and the sounding-right are simultaneously matters of the sensual body of the poem—which is, to a degree, a matter of what I used to call technique—and matters of the spiritual validity of the image—the truth to the unconscious content of the ancient world inside each of us moving up through the images and into the poem. And once this is embodied in the poem, then it is possible that through the noises, the line breaks, the rhythms—which are *always* talking—and through the mysterious content of the image—that one inside can communicate with another.

I think you are the only member of your generation to have known Eliot, Pound, Frost, and Dylan Thomas.

Maybe so.

Would you comment on the experience of having known these men—their influence if any and your reaction?

So much of the world around us, whether we're in school, or with our families, or whatever, tries to tell us, "Don't take yourself so seriously." This is the standard protective device of most of humanity most of the time. We are born bored; we die bored; what difference does it make? If you're going to struggle to try to make an art, you know perfectly well that you may spend your whole life working at something and ultimately failing. *But*, you have the example of the people who have made the struggle anyway, and who in your mind have done something good. This in itself is a force opposite that bourgeois force that says, "Don't take yourself so seriously." The example of the poets says, "It's all right.

Try it. You may make it, you may not. What matters is the doing."

When you grow up, you tend to think of life as a slope, up a hill, at the top of which there is a plateau; there is some point at which you have made it in whatever you are trying to do. Then you know that you are good and you walk on a horizontal plane thereafter. Well, I know the name of that horizontal plane. It is death. It's the end. The only possible way to stay alive, the only possible name of being alive, is "continue the struggle." I remember Dylan Thomas telling me when he was thirty-eight, a year before he died, that he didn't think he was very good—that he had written maybe three poems that he liked. One was the poem on his thirtieth birthday, one was the poem on his thirty-fifth birthday, and one he called "an early Hardyish piece," "This Bread I Break." That's the way he felt that night. Another time, there might have been no poems, or twenty-five poems, or three entirely different poems.

All of these men felt that their lives were a matter of their daily consideration, that their life's work was, at each point in time, breaking against the shore of the moment. It is always possible to change it all, suddenly to make the breakthrough, suddenly to be *really good*.

You saw T. S. Eliot when you went to England for the first time. What was the conversation like?

I had actually met him first in America, briefly, at a party. He asked me to drop around and see him at Faber and Faber when I got to England. Of course, I was spooked out of my mind. He also suggested that I might show him some of my poems. He spoke about them a bit, rather kindly, pointing out one or two places where the poems were bad. He was a generous man.

We also talked about our literary generations in a way that makes me feel very pompous in restrospect. I was twenty-three. I was frightened of him and didn't really realize his humor, which was constant. He was *always* playful in talk, and frequently in his most serious poems, for that matter.

What about your experience with Ezra Pound?

My experience with Pound was limited in time. I went down to Rome in 1960 (he was staying in Rome at the apartment of friends), in order to do an interview for the *Paris Review*. I'd been planning to go to see him in Washington when he was at Saint Elizabeth's, but I never got around to it. I was frightened of him too—as someone who had ideas which I didn't like and whom I thought would be unfriendly. What I found was, in fact, an extraordinarily lonely man. He wanted companionship. My wife and I went out to dinner with him several times. He wanted us around all the time: he wanted to talk. He was cordial, friendly, and extremely worried about his own mental state—not about insanity so much as loss of power, loss of creativity. When we were doing the interview, he constantly feared that he sounded too tired, that he could not finish the sentences that he'd begun. He eventually did finish them. Sometimes a sentence would begin one day and conclude two days later. It was a strange time. When I wasn't interviewing him and we were just talking, he felt more energetic. There was less demand on him.

On the last day of the interview, he jumbled around in some suitcases at the end of the room and took out drafts of cantos on which he was working and sat down on the sofa with me and said, "Are they any good?

Tell me. Do you think I should go on?" I read them and tried to tell him what I thought of them, just as straight as I could, because I wouldn't lie to that man or try to tell him anything about his poems that I didn't believe. The fragments were superb. But I did not know if he could go on, because of his health.

Once I was waiting for him in a cafe across from the apartment where he was staying. I had been there before and the waiter knew me. The waiter knew him separately. Pound came in and sat with me. The waiter came over and made the connection and said a sentence in Italian which ended with the word "figlio." Pound looked over at me and then back at the waiter and said, "Si, si."

Well, I felt like that temporarily—like his son. He felt at that time that he'd been, for so much of his life, mistaken. It was sad, but it was also triumphant that he could have the strength *and* the humility to think that, perhaps, he had been mistaken. I'm speaking of mistakes of idea—that's what he was speaking of—mistakes to do with politics, to do with fascism, and also mistakes to do with the intellectual structure of the *Cantos*. He used to say—he said it several times—that perhaps he had been mistaken in putting Confucius at the top of Paradise; it should have been Agassiz. He was, of course, greatly troubled by these doubts. Here was his life's work, incomplete and perhaps wrong . . . and he questioned his strength about going on.

Is that possibility—the possibility of these great poets in any era when poetry was so volatile, so changing—is it possible now for that type of effect to happen again in poetry? It seems to me that the external circumstances have so altered with the incredible political messes we're in, the sense of prevailing disaster, the wars . . .

Art still exists by itself, aside from social change. We know that a language can cease to exist and that any poetry which survives will be part of a dead language. We know, as Yeats says in "Lapis Lazuli," that sculpture and art are destroyed. We have not only the sense of our own death, which men have always had, but the sense of the death, even the death of our civilization, even the death of our species. And although it is reasonable to acknowledge that with the death of the species, all art is dead, I think that to many of us art is the bulwark against this extinction. Art is created against death.

It's a bulwark, but it's not a conservative thing. It preserves the spirit of a person who created and wrote it to an extent that his times, his people, his language are preserved. However, it is radical in the sense that it will represent the values of the world being born, if there will be a new birth.

And if there will be a new birth in the world, now, I believe that what is happening in the world of poetry will be a leading part of that birth. That birth will come from the dark spirit which moves inside us. We will survive by going beyond the rational, not by suppressing it, not by destroying the machine, which is childishness, but by going beyond this in the wholeness of our lives towards the mystery at the center. Some people have always known about it. Priests and poets.

In the first edition of New *Poets of England and America, why did you leave out the Black Mountain group, Creeley and others? It seems unusual, to say the least, since you indicated earlier that you take a serious interest in promoting poetry.*

It's ridiculous, but we did not acknowledge that they existed, and we weren't reading them. I speak for myself anyway. They were printing; the magazines were there.

I know that I avoided looking at the magazines because I had decided that the stuff was really no good without opening up my mind to it.

Obviously, I wanted to keep my mind closed. I thought I *knew* how to write poetry; I *knew* what to do; I didn't want anybody upsetting me. This was silly and cowardly, but it's how I acted. I had met Robert Creeley when I was an undergraduate and we had one long and good talk. Then I'd read some of his stuff in a magazine (I can't remember which magazine) and it was like e. e. cummings. I remember thinking, "Oh, Creeley's just a cummings imitator." Later, when his style changed, I didn't read him. He was in magazines, the pamphlets were around, but I didn't read them. So, I think that the parochialism of the first edition of *New Poets of England and America* was a result of a kind of *careful* ignorance.

I want to come back to some of your early assessments of poetry in America. You talked of your failure to see the Black Mountain group. If I read correctly, you had a deep distrust of the Beats also.

Sure. You see, two things are going on in any failure to recognize excellence when it first happens. One of them is that you have an idea of what poetry is; this is true whether you are being a critic or being a poet or both. You're *set*; when something new comes along, instead of having the imagination or the energy to accommodate yourself to it, the easier thing is to deny it and to say that it's not poetry, it's no good. This is what happened to Wordsworth when he published *Lyrical Ballads*. This accounts for some of my planned ignorance when new things began to happen in the late 1950s.

But there was also another thing; my own fear of

poetry, my own fear of the looseness of the imagination, my fear of fantasy. Most of this new poetry was not fantastic, but a lot of it was considerably more loose and less conventional than mine, especially in intellectual and spiritual ways. So I feared the poetry not only because it attacked my stylistic set, but also because it was a danger to my *emotional* set. Learning to read some of this poetry has been a liberation to me. I think of Allen Ginsberg, among others, although as my own writing has changed, I don't think it has come to resemble Allen's.

In 1961, while reviewing for the Nation, *you wrote that the most disconcerting thing about modernism had been its discontinuity. Using Olson's essay on "Projective Verse," you alluded to his comment that the time has come to pick "the fruits of the experiments of Cummings, Pound, Williams." Has American poetry been harvesting these fruits lately?*

Not these fruits. I didn't know so much about modernism then as I do now. The strange thing in English and American poetry, with exceptions that are hardly worth noticing, is that it was separate from international modernism. In international modernism there was a continuity in style among painters, sculptors, poets, playwrights from Latin America to Cuba to Spain to Germany to Russia (around the time of the revolution) to France, Greece, and Scandinavia.

English and American modern poetry, while some of it is excellent, is really quite separate. The movement that Olson was talking about was not a single movement but a series of eccentric acts by people writing alone out of their own reading and experience. It did not have the inwardness that is common to German expressionism and to "modernismo" in the Spanish language and which is also common to expressionist and surrealist painting.

In the last ten years or so, American poetry has joined international modernism. It has not harvested the fruits of Pound and Williams, it has harvested the fruits of the great early painters of this century and of the poets from Spain and France and Germany who had something in common with these painters.

Yes. That's part of what one recognizes in, for example, Bly's The Sixties *with its emphasis on the poetry of Neruda.*

Bly is the single, most important innovator—or transmitter—of this particular energy. Other people have come to similar positions independently. It had to happen. Even most of the descendents of the Pound and Williams tradition, not just the descendents of Lowell and Wilbur, for instance, seem to me to have moved in a general way toward the poetry of fantasy.

Incidentally, when Robert Bly and I were undergraduates together at college, we were tremendously iambic. We were poets of the fifties and Bob was writing blank verse narratives and sonnets. When I was at Oxford just after college, Bob sent me a bundle of Shakespearean sonnets he had been working on for a long time. Even before I could answer him, and tell him what I thought of them, I had a letter from him saying that this was no use; it was too old fashioned; he couldn't write this way now. He had begun to change. We all went through enormous changes. He led the way, for many of us.

At the same time at Harvard when Bob and I were undergraduates (we met when I was a freshman and he was a sophomore), there was John Ashbery, Frank O'Hara, Kenneth Koch. Also there was L. E. Sissman, Adrienne Rich, and Peter Davison. Sissman was in a class with me, and I dated Adrienne a couple of times. Richard Wilbur, a little older, was a Junior Fellow. Robert Creeley had just left Harvard, but he was around the area, and some of us met him. Certainly Creeley was not being iambic! Koch and Ashbery, while seeming a little Audenish then, were beginning to write a poetry of fantasy and strangeness—certainly more than Bly and I were at that time.

How did your poetry change?

The old way ran out. I found myself afflicted with a sense of the staleness and glibness of my verse. The forms were predictable, the feelings were superficial, the wit was easy. I had to put it aside. I flailed around. I worked with other techniques, like syllabics and eventually free verse. But it was really a searching for the poetry of spiritual freedom. I discovered that by telling a lie—by telling what is, in outward terms, a lie—we express something which is true inside ourselves. I am speaking of the dream self which is always within us, even when we are awake. In this dream place, things we fear the most are true, and things we desire the most are true. When we express these things, we are telling outward lies. We may say, as I said in a poem that I wrote when I was young, that "the snow hangs still in the middle of the air." You invent such a place because you *want* it to exist, because you dread mutability, because you don't want to die, or grow older, or break up with the girl.

This place has existed in poetry from the beginning. So I wrote a poetry of fantasy, on occasion, when I was in my teens and in my twenties. But for a period in my mid-twenties, I became more aware of what I was doing with fantasy, and I was frightened of it. I courted the poetry of rationality, a poetry in which illusion was defeated, and in which reason asserted its supremacy.

But gradually, from my late twenties on, I have been able to allow the dream self to come up and take its place in my poems. Partly, this came from reading other poems, and partly from accepting parts of myself which I wanted to cover up before. I was able to begin to write poems in which I had no idea of what I was talking about. When I was twenty-five years old, I wouldn't have dreamed of writing a poem in which I didn't know what I was talking about. Or in which I didn't *think* I knew what I was talking about. In the poems from that time which are any good, there is always something going on of which I was not aware. The topside—which I was aware of—is still there, of course; but the underside, which I concealed from myself, is the power that makes the engine go.

In recent years, I have come to accept the beginning of a poem, or even a whole draft, without the slightest clue to the subject matter. Words come to me heavy with emotion, and I accept them even though I have no idea what they are trying to tell me. The first poem I remember writing in this way is my musk-ox poem, "The Long River." In 1958, I remember, I began it with a phrase about a musk-ox. I had no idea where it came from. I trusted it, because it came heavy with feeling. For perhaps two years I lived with these phrases, as the poem began to extend itself down the page. It doesn't extend very long, as a matter of fact. But it took me a long time to write it.

The process of writing a poem is a process of developing and shaping the words which the poem begins with, until finally, upon completion of the poem, or perhaps after completion, you can see what it is that you are expressing. The poem is a vehicle for self-discovery. Of course the premise upon which this kind of poetry is based is that if you discover something that is deep enough inside yourself, it's going to be a part of other people's insides, too, and reveal themselves to themselves.

Many of us, then, went through a movement from a poetry which was formal in its meter and rhyme and which had a rational and external narrative, to poetry which is free verse with improvised forms and improvised resolutions of noise—and which is more intimate, more emotional, and more irrational. I don't see why there should be a necessary connection between free verse and the poetry of fantasy. It seems to me that, in my case, the *associations* of iambic verse were rational. The iambic poem stated a problem and solved it, and tied it up neatly at the end, like a little bundle. It seems to me that I was unable to break through that neatness of content until I was able to move into the form—free verse—where I had no illusion of control. When I am writing a poem now, I don't know, when I am writing the first line, what the next line is going to be like. I don't know what sound it's going to make. I improvise until it sounds right and feels right. Ultimately, for me, the poem has to feel resolved and whole and single and fixed and unmovable. Yeats used to say that the finished poem made a sound like the click of the lid of a perfectly made box. I still hear that click in free verse as well as I ever did in the sonnet. You improvise toward the click.

You have been talking about some of your early poems. That first book, Exiles and Marriages, *was a huge success.*

It was in 1955, I think. What do you think accounted for the success?

Probably the large quantity of bad verse in it. I was blessed with the praises of *Time*. They printed my picture and did a review of it—something they don't do very often with a first book or poems by a young poet. And, of course, it was a curse.

There are a lot of poems in there that seem to me to come out of the fear of poetry, and which seem to me accommodating to the bourgeoisie. They were mostly poems of the rational period I was talking about. They tell you it's all right to have illusions, but you'd better get over them because, after all, reality is reality. Or they tell you to praise virtue and blame vice, or at least to be nice and guilty over being vicious. Three-quarters of it is without any interest whatsoever. There are a few poems that I like all through. Others are partly OK. Recently, when I did the selection for *The Alligator Bride*, I was able to revise and improve some of the old ones, and reprint them.

You once wrote that "the true artist refines his feeling and thought in revision until he finds the absolute shape and motion which satisfy him." Do you still revise heavily or do you rely on spontaneous experience to determine the poem's shape?

I revise heavily. Usually, it takes a long time. This isn't, of course, a necessity for anybody else. Some friends of mine will work on the same poem steadily for eighteen or twenty hours. I might take two years to finish the poem, and put in eighteen or twenty hours during the two years. I work on the poem for a while, make a few changes, cross out a few things, make a few comments in the margin perhaps, and after a few minutes I can't stand to look at it any more. I put it away. The next day, the next week, or the next month, I'll come back to it again and get at it. I have never written a poem in one draft which has remained the same. I have had a few experiences where a poem has become *nearly* whole. Very few. However, it still took me six or eight months to make the two tiny changes that made the poems come out right.

You asked in your question, "Do you revise heavily or do you rely on spontaneous experience?" Well, I refuse the question, because I *do* revise a lot and I *do* rely on the spontaneous. The revision is spontaneous. I look at the poem which has seemed fixed to me, and suddenly I see that a part of it is wrong. I quickly cross out what I don't like—I've made something new.

It happens, also, when I'm not looking at the poem. I may be walking down the street and a line will come into my head—not a revision of an old line, perhaps, but a line that is brand new—I recognize that it belongs to a certain poem. I have been working on the poem all the time without knowing it. I'll write it down somewhere and later, back at my house, I'll look at the draft of the poem and see where my new line fits. Or if it fits.

Sometimes when I read a poem aloud at a reading, I find myself making a mistake. If I make a mistake, I listen to it, because my mistake may be what I really should put there. Or it may simply show that I don't really like the line.

I suppose I tend to revise more by deletion than by anything else. I have an original image which develops into a whole draft of the poem—sometimes at one sitting, more often over a period of time. Then the long process of getting it right is often the process of finding out what to omit. Deletion is at least as creative as addition. I tend to explain too much. I tend to go into too much detail. And this over-explaining and this detail are not just technical matters, or ideas about what a poem *ought* to be. These over-statements are a device by which I hold down the feeling, hold it at arm's length through explanation or elaboration. It takes me a long time to come to the clarity and intensity of the single thrust of the feeling. The upper regions of my head, where the words begin to come in from the feelings, are still concerned *not* to see, *not* to understand, *not* to admit.

I was reading this morning an essay of yours called "The Vatic Voice," in which you talk about the way in which a poem surfaces. I wonder if you would talk about that now?

Sure. The "Vatic Voice" is not a phrase I'm too fond of, although I made it up. Often, poems begin in a passive way, a phrase comes to me, or some words come to me. I overhear something inside myself. This happens in certain moods. The beginnings come to me in little meteor showers—a day or two, perhaps two weeks—I will have many new ideas. Everything I look at seems to bloom with poetry. During the same period, I make a lot of mistakes when I'm talking. Freudian slips, and so on. I find myself saying weird things in conversation—things I had no idea I was going to say, metaphorical things usually. There seems to be a kind of alleyway down to the unconscious mind. I'm a bit schizoid, I guess, but I feel all right. Mysterious things surface more clearly. During these periods, when I am not with people, I daydream very loosely. Unlike the night dream, I can watch it—I can listen to it. I hear the voice, speaking and delivering sorts of messages. Certain phrases stick with me.

They have power—emotional power—and they have intensity. These phrases may become parts of poems or clues to poems or directions toward poems. However, this voice is not always available: laziness and undirected activity sometimes seem to help it to come. But I've had the experience of going through a period like this when I was enormously *busy*. There was one time about a year ago when there was a period of ten days or two weeks before I went into the hospital for an operation. I had to do three poetry readings and meet a deadline on an article early, because I knew I was going to be sick. Also, I was teaching. I was frantic. But during that period ten or twelve poems happened—the first drafts happened. I'm working on them. Some of them are still in notebooks and hardly worked over at all. I remember writing in the backs of books in airport limousines, writing at 30,000 feet, writing in motels. So much was happening. This was the reverse of the usual quietness or laziness. Really, I can't make any rules for the conditions under which I hear this voice.

In your own work, I see a change from the highly optimistic, almost cheerful poetry of Exiles and Marriages *to a more sober poetry—a poetry, really, of grief. How do you feel about it?*

In the first place, I think that a lot of the cheerful and optimistic poetry of *Exiles and Marriages* is fakey. Some of it is simply naive. In either case, it is bad.

Of course there is a poetry of high spirits which can be honest and true. I think I've written some of that even recently. A new poem like "Happy Times" in *The Alligator Bride* seems to me to be full of good cheer. That's fine; I've nothing against high spirits as long as a poem is true.

There are a few poems of grief in *Exiles*, like the elegy for my grandfather. But real grief started in *The Dark Houses*, mostly. My father died about the time *Exiles and Marriages* was published. I learned that he was going to die on the day the publisher accepted the book. *Dark Houses* begins with a poem on my father's death. A poem I still like. (I revised it a little for *The Alligator Bride*.) As I look back at *The Dark Houses* as a whole, it seems to me that the whole book is an angry elegy over his death. Though I don't think too much of the book as a whole, it is more honest than *Exiles and Marriages*, partly because it deals openly with unpleasant subject matter. Its failure lies in a muting of these feelings—not a changing or a perversion of them, but a tendency toward gray understatement.

I would like to be able to write poetry out of any mood. I feel that unhappy poetry—poetry that comes out of the situation of grief or loss or anger—tends to be stronger than poetry of the light heart. I think there is a valid reason for this in the nature of the art and in the nature of the poetic process.

This is what I mean. Energy comes from conflict. The sensual body of the poem is pleasure. A poem has a body which gives pleasure—the sounds of it, the weight of it. The poem, no matter what its subject matter—no matter how terrifying or anxious—has its separate existence as a pleasurable object. It has an existence like a stone which a sculptor has worked over. If you are writing a poem out of pleasurable feelings, the theme-pleasure walks hand in hand with the sense-pleasure of the poem. But it can go only a short distance because there is no conflict to give energy. On the other hand, if you are writing a poem out of grief and loss, or out of anger, the side of the poem which is its sensual body moves in conflict with the pain of the content. You move, then, from one thing to the other, consistently. You move from thesis to antithesis to synthesis, and then the same thing over again. The constant movement, which is so quick as to seem simultaneous, between the pleasure of the body and the pain of the spirit in loss, conflicts and lends energy by this conflict.

In A Roof of Tiger Lilies *you have several poems on the barrenness of American life. "The Wives," for example. Is your more recent poetry perhaps an attempt to raise the more sensitive garden?*

Those are terms in which I sometimes think of the new poetry. The second book was called *Dark Houses* and the third *A Roof of Tiger Lilies*. The color comes into it. If you look through the books, there is a movement from dark colors, which are arid and which represent sterility, to a poetry which looks to an alternative to *The Dark Houses*, which is bright colors and flowers. There is a poem in *A Roof of Tiger Lilies* called "Digging" which is about wanting to become bright flowers.

In that elegy for my father that began *The Dark Houses*, I was talking about darkness and sterility and the grief and loss. I said in that poem, "This love is jail; another sets us free." The other love which "sets us free" was only referred to in that book; it didn't happen. I did not plot out my life and say "Now I am going to go after the other side," but, in fact, I think I have been doing it. I prefer pleasure to pain, which doesn't make me very unusual. Bright colors are pleasure. But the search for the yellow flower is a search for a fulfillment of the self and the whole body which will come to grief both in the idiomatic sense and in the sense of the straight abstraction. Within the poem—within the poet— there is a conflict between the desire to let the impulses free, and the almost continual necessary frustration of these desires. The frustration is partly the punishment we impose upon ourselves for liberating our impulses. It is a self-enclosed circle, and one cannot escape. Still, the search for the yellow flower is the only way.

One of the things that I concerned myself with when I began to read your work was the rendering of image. In some of your earlier poems, the thing that amazed me was the way in which you avoided sensual identifications that can be literally rendered as a "scene." Rather, you tend to excise the literal images out until what remains is an interpreted sensual image. I think particularly of "The Long River." Are you aware of having avoided the literal sensual renderings in your poems—in order to avoid the explicit statement?

I try to avoid the literal statement in general, not just in the rendering of scenes. In poems explicitness is a way of holding experience at arm's length. There are erotic poems in which I originally wrote detail almost with diagrams. I had an impulse early on, in the process of revision, to cut out some of the physiology. But I hesitated, at first, for fear that I was censoring myself, or being merely prudish. Eventually, I came to realize, with a little help from my friends, that the physiological detail had the effect of cutting down the eroticism. The more pornographic they were, the less erotic they were. I have been able, I think, to cut out the specific physiological terms to a great extent, and to retain the action and the spirit, so that the poem is more emotional.

Mr. Hall, two poems have particularly impressed me— one which I mentioned before is "The Long River," and the other is "The Alligator Bride." In both cases these strike me as surrealist poems. In most of your poems, the material is outward, poems like "The Days." But in both "The Long River" and "The Alligator Bride" you seem to go inside or down deeply into an interior world. Do you sense this also?

In a poem like "The Days" or "The Table" there is a scene-setting, an outside, but the intensity of the poetry comes from fantasy—after the scene has been established. The movement inward to the emotional situation requires fantasy, or surrealist imagery. But the outside has been a necessary lead towards the inside. The layers of discourse are partially separated in poems like this. It is true that I enjoy and am most excited by poems like "The Long River," "The Alligator Bride," "The Blue Wing," and "Happy Times" in which there *is* no topside—or the topside is nonsensical or absurd or tells a story that makes no sense—and in which all of the coherence and all of the unity is emotional and underneath. This is the kind of poem which excites me the most, from which I learn the most and which pleases me the most, because I feel less control and more discovery. Yet, I don't want to make rules for myself and say that this is the only kind of poem that I will write.

Is the surrealist poem for you a comfortable poem? Does it seem to you that the surrealist poem is more suited to the times?

I can't say that I'm conscious of what kinds of poems are more suited to the times. Looking at the body of work being done in America right now, it would seem that the surrealist poem is suited to the times, because we are making it so. I don't know.

I find that whatever I write, if I am able to go through

with it and complete it there is a comfort in the composition—a comfort in the resolution of the whole. Since there is more anxiety connected with the surrealist poem (we are not aware of the nature of the material as we shape it) there is consequently more comfort in the resolution of that anxiety. You are getting something under control that is hidden and mysterious and sometimes violent. You are able to control it in the sense that you form it—but not in the sense that you take the claws out of its paws.

In many of your selected poems from previous volumes which you use in The Alligator Bride, *I sense a dramatic new compression—a tightening to the barest essentials, almost a restriction to a single emotional effect. Does this new work represent a significant new change to you? Does it look forward to your new material?*

I cannot look forward to my new material. At the point where something is changing, I am aware that there is a change but I don't know what I am doing. Once I understand what I have been doing, it's used up. I must go on to something else. In the process of making a new group of poems, which may be the work of a year or two—I work on families of poems at the same time—only gradually do I become aware of what I am doing. I cannot tell you where I am going to go; I can only tell you where I have been.

In the first part of your question, were you talking about the revisions of the older poems?

Yes.

There the compression seems to me, to pick up your word, not a *restriction*, but a *liberation*. I think that when I cut something out, it was something which was restricting the poem either by saying too much or by explaining too much. And the act of cutting, for me, loosens the poem and gets rid of the dead weight so it can fly. I feel this with some of the poems I wrote many years ago, from which I was able simply to excerpt a stanza, like "My Son, My Executioner." The first poem in the book is "Wedding Party," a poem I began when I was nineteen. It seems to me vastly improved by omitting a middle stanza which was absolutely worthless. I didn't realize until a year ago when I was finishing the text of the selected poems, with the help of a friend, that the middle stanza was perfectly extra. The poem is more powerful by leaving it out. Sometimes these extra stanzas are simply the results of diffidence. You don't have enough confidence in your images, so you want to explain them.

Much of your work was filled with images of airplanes. Could you comment on the significance of these images?

When I was growing up, airplanes were still fairly new. I was born not long after Lindbergh flew the Atlantic and my mother and father were born in the year of Kitty Hawk. I saved pictures of airplanes in scrapbooks. I knew every plane in the sky. I still do. Planes have been terribly important to me as things in themselves. I love to fly. And then, again and again, in my poetry, and even in my conversation when I am reaching around for a metaphor or an analogy, I find myself using flying and airplanes.

I think that at different times these images embody any number of things. Mostly my airplanes—in my poems—are crashed. The first poem which I ever published in the *Harvard Advocate* when I was a freshman (a poem I never reprinted) was about an airplane crash. The most recent airplane poem is the first from which there has been a survivor. Somebody said it was a sign of maturity.

There are other images of stopped machinery, the locomotive lost in the woods, the abandoned automobile, and even the image of empty and decaying houses. There are certainly embodied, in all these images, feelings of loss, death, deprivation, and abandonment.

Do you think this is a common procedure for poets to have fixed symbolic values in a certain sense? David Ignatow, for instance, does it with knives.

It's not a procedure. I don't know if they are "fixed symbolic values." They are more likely over-determined images.

Could you explain what you mean by over-determined images?

I am not sure I am using that phrase correctly. As I understand it, an image is over-determined when it derives a power, in excess of what you would rationally expect it to have, from being the locus of a number of *different* sources of power in your psyche.

I think many poets, if you look through their work, have certain sets that come up again and again and again. Obviously, in Yeats, there are a certain number of words—like the moon—which recur frequently. And you cannot fix a particular meaning to it, because at one point the moon may be an image for the aging process, for going down towards death—in "Adam's Curse"; yet more frequently it's an image of the imagination and of the world of darkness inside yourself—"Lines Written in Dejection." The word always emerges with power, but the particular association is granted by the particular context.

Some of your airplane poems have skeletons in the cockpits. Today, after we had talked about these poems last night, you showed me an article from the morning paper which reported that a World War II plane had been found in the Philippines in which there were two skeletons. How does this make you feel?

The shivers run down my spine again. I read it in the paper after having talked with you about this theme, after having talked about the theme in conversation a thousand times, after having written about it in my poetry—and now when I read it in the paper, it happens all over again. The shivers. There is something more here than I have ever reached. In this particular news item, what struck me and touched me particularly were the dog tags which they found on the skeletons with the names and service numbers—something preserved out of all this time. The plane had crashed there more than twenty-five years ago.

Is this, again, part of the sense of loss you are talking about?

I suppose loss—and abandonment. I think that sometimes, at any rate, the sense of the crash of the airplane is associated with an abandonment that has to do with women. (Really, I think I know more than I am telling you. I don't want to tell you.) Certainly this is true in a poem which I like especially, "The Blue Wing." I think that for all of us, in the deepest place, all women are one woman.

What is the loss which the skeleton in the cockpit has experienced?

There are two poems—"The Blue Wing" and "The Man in the Dead Machine"—and there are two different losses. I cannot fix the loss any more than the poems fix it. I just talked about "The Blue Wing"'s sense of loss as connected, in some way, with women. In the other poem there is some of that too, because when I was writing about the plane in the jungle, I said that it was covered with vines "as thick as arms." Two things happen in that image which are developed throughout the poem, though I was not aware of either one of them at the time of writing the phrase. The feeling is like being caught in a web—like a fly in a spider's web. It is also like being held in the arms . . . of the mother. These senses may be seen as contradictory, but they are two ways of looking at the same thing. You are comforted and cradled in those arms, but at the same time you are stuck and you have to get out. The getting out and the getting away from the arms, which is necessary for your life, leaves many of us perpetually with the sense of the loss of those arms.

But the image which you use, in "The Man in the Dead Machine," is more profound. It is really the skeleton, the body stripped of its flesh. It is death.

That is right. When I was writing that poem, I thought of it in a more superficial way than I do now—now that I see what it really does. (A young poet pointed it out to me, in fact.) I thought I was writing about the sense of being stuck or paralyzed (dead) in the midst of life. But really, the poem has that permanent sense of the skull beneath the skin, the potential death in us all. Here the airplane and the skeleton are different. "The Blue Wing" is not at all about the skull beneath the skin. As far as *I* know.

You've already talked about one theme in your work— the longing for sensual pleasure. There are, of course, others. One is the grief for old people who die, and another is an awareness, often frightening, of organic movement inside the body towards death. Poems like "The Repeated Shapes" and "By the Exeter River" are examples of the first. "My Son, My Executioner" and "Mount Kearsarge" are examples of the latter.

I have felt connected with old people more than any of my friends here. I remember thinking from an early age of the coming deaths of people I loved. I suppose it must go back to something before my grandfather, and I don't understand it. When I was nine years old, a great aunt died. I remember lying in bed repeating to myself, insistently, and melodramatically, "Now death has become a reality." I wanted to insist upon it, to know it, and not to turn away from it. I was morbid. I also remember touching the hand of an old great-uncle, a minister in New Hampshire, and realizing that after my fingers pressed into the flesh of his hand, his flesh did not respond immediately, it was not resilient. The flesh very gradually moved out again. I did it over and over again, knowing that what I was touching was dying flesh. I wanted to know that.

I think that I loved them because they were going to die. That sounds simple and direct enough, and yet I am suspicious of it as a whole story. Did I, perhaps, want them to die? Did I, perhaps, in some way love death or want to die myself, and therefore associate myself with them? I really cannot answer. What was the second part of your question?

I mentioned the apparent theme of organic movement inside the body towards death, which you seem partly to be dealing with now. I mentioned the poem, "My Son, My Executioner."

"Sleeping" is an example of that.

"My Son, My Executioner" was written when my son was born. I was twenty-five, and I had the sense of his replacing me, and, therefore, of my own necessary death. But this is only the top of the poem. It is *there*, but other things are going on as well. To look upon your son as your executioner is not the friendliest way to look at him. There seems to be anger in the poem. But why would I be mad at this little baby that I loved to hold and to feed? It was many years before I saw something else about that poem. (I imagine lots of other people have seen it, because they didn't have reasons *not* to see it.) A year or two ago, when my son was about fourteen, he said to me, "That poem you wrote about me when I was born, that's really about you and your daddy, isn't it?" Of course, he's right. "My Son, My Executioner" is much more a memory of my feelings toward my own father than it is, actually, about me and my baby son. Having a baby son apparently reminded me of the feelings toward the father which every man must have, the wish to take the father's place with the mother. The poem contains a sense that my body is moving on towards death, but I think it probably takes most of its power from the wish that my father move on toward death. (He died a year and a half later.) Part of me, in a primitive way, wanted him to die, and of course was guilty about it. The energy, I think, comes from this conflict of desire and guilt over desire.

Since we're talking about that early period again, what kind of satisfaction did you get from writing the reminiscences of String Too Short to Be Saved? *How did it differ from your poetry?*

Writing that book of prose memoirs of New Hampshire was a tremendous satisfaction, a deep swim into memory. Writing it was relaxing compared to poetry, because I could let the images proliferate. I could go on and on remembering and inventing out of memory. You know the scene, the place, the feel, the smell—and you invent a day. You know the way people talk; so then you make up things for them to say. It is a reenactment of the past by ventriloquism. You drift down into memory and people it, make it talk, feel the sun on your back and the wind in your hair.

Writing it also released things for me, I think. I wrote some poems directly out of it. I'd be writing along in prose and I would get excited about some images, so I'd stop writing the prose, pick up another piece of paper, and begin to write in lines, with tighter control over rhythm, and I suppose more conciseness. But much more important than that, I think the book helped me to open up to feeling, to acknowledge feeling more. Writing that book led to the gradual increase in intensity of feeling that there is in *A Roof of Tiger Lilies*, which I was writing at that time.

The writer's relationship to his own past is fantastically important. Typically, writers have good memories. They are constantly going over things and remembering. People have said that everything truly important in your life happens before you are fifteen or sixteen. We go over this material, reassemble it, put it together again and again. By the act of writing down a part of my life which I seemed able to preserve, and from which I could recall strong feeling, clearly and cleanly—I opened myself to the possibility of writing other feelings from other scenes and parts of my life. *String Too Short to Be Saved* was an exercise in unclogging passages.

So long as we're talking about the shift in emphasis—of being able to deal with other aspects of your experience—would you comment on your new work? Where does it seem to be heading? What new winds are moving it?

The new poems in *The Alligator Bride* were written from January of 1966 through April or May of 1969. I began some of them earlier, but I had two years when I couldn't write at all, from the winter of 1964 until January 3rd, 1966. Images came to me which I wrote down in notebooks, but I couldn't put them together. I lacked the quietness, the serenity, where things can combine in your head and grow and move. All I had was little flashes of images. I could take notation in my head, but I couldn't combine things. I was able, in that bad time, to write other things. I wrote some journalism, and put together a play. But I couldn't write poetry—the most important thing to me. I was denying that to myself.

After two years, which were terrible years, I began to be able to combine images again. It seems to me that I was able then to get through to a more dangerous and scary feeling than I had before. The example that comes to mind is "The Alligator Bride," which I worked on within the first six months of beginning to write again.

To acknowledge these feelings, to bring them out, and to give them shape and form, was something I certainly could not have done ten years before. I don't think I did it so strongly in the poems of *A Roof of Tiger Lilies*, either. A part of me had been holding back, you see, from the acknowledgment of the whole thing. Perhaps there is still some holding back, and I wonder if the humor, or whatever it is, in "The Alligator Bride," is itself a device by which I am trying to palliate the misery in the poem. I don't know.

I am mainly interested in trying to write a poem in which, as Galway Kinnell said to me in conversation last fall, you bring everything that you have done, everything that you know, together all at once. That's not quoting Galway exactly, that's what I got from what he said. That kind of poem involves knowing yourself. You have to be able to get at the truth of your feeling and not to distort it. This is where I want to go now, and where I hope I am going.

Note: "The Man in the Dead Machine" appears on page 76.

Poems Mentioned in this Interview

My Son, My Executioner

My son, my executioner,
    I take you in my arms,
Quiet and small and just astir,
    And whom my body warms.

Sweet death, small son, our instrument
    Of immortality,
Your cries and hungers document
    Our bodily decay.

We twenty-five and twenty-two,
    Who seemed to live forever,
Observe enduring life in you
    And start to die together.

.

The Long River

The musk-ox smells
in his long head
my boat coming. When
I feel him there,
intent, heavy,

the oars make wings
in the white night,
and deep woods are close
on either side
where trees darken.

I rowed past towns
in their black sleep
to come here. I rowed
by northern grass
and cold mountains.

The musk-ox moves
when the boat stops,
in hard thickets. Now
the wood is dark
with old pleasures.

The Alligator Bride

The clock of my days winds down.
The cat eats sparrows outside my window.
Once, she brought me a small rabbit
which we devoured together, under
the Empire Table
while the men shrieked
repossessing the gold umbrella.

Now the beard on my clock turns white.
My cat stares into dark corners
missing her gold umbrella.
She is in love
with the Alligator Bride.

Ah, the tiny fine white
teeth! The Bride, propped on her tail
in white lace
stares from the holes
of her eyes. Her stuck-open mouth
laughs at minister and people.

On bare new wood
fourteen tomatoes,
a dozen ears of corn,
six bottles of white wine,
a melon,
a cat,
broccoli
and the Alligator Bride.

The color of bubble gum,
the consistency of petroleum jelly,
wickedness oozes
from the palm of my left hand.
My cat licks it.
I watch the Alligator Bride.

Big houses like shabby boulders
hold themselves tight
in gelatin.
I am unable to daydream.
The sky is a gun aimed at me.
I pull the trigger.
The skull of my promises
leans in a black closet, gapes
with its good mouth
for a teat to suck.

A bird flies back and forth
in my house that is covered by gelatin
and the cat leaps at it
missing. Under the Empire Table
the Alligator Bride
lies in her bridal shroud.
My left hand
leaks on the Chinese carpet.

Happy Times

There is straw in the goose bindery.
Egg princesses hear
tiny electric feet of sample witches
in the white city of bacon.
Tongues, tongues, they grow on the porch.

Mattresses lumber through the Simian Quarter,
ablaze. "Karen, the walnuts
are bothering me!" The caboose dwindles
which I fabricated of worn fruit punch.
I have eaten the fur hats.

Buick of yellow leaves, sing the peanut wheel!
While the fiddle dances
to the newspaper that regards it,
the smiles of important shrimp
shine like motors in the cabbage light.

Questions from *The Review*

On the occasion of its tenth anniversary, the English magazine *The Review* asked two questions of many "poets, critics and editors, both English and American . . .":

1. *What, in your view, have been the most (a) encouraging, (b) discouraging features of the poetry scene during the past decade?*

2. *What developments do you hope to see during the next decade?*

Here are some answers:

Geoffrey Hill is the best poet in England. It is discouraging that some people do not seem aware of his work.

English poetry is a million particles spinning apart from each other. Little groups gather like gnats, but a wind disperses them. So much anger, so much bitchery, so much attention to reviews, to the Arts Council, to allegiances and betrayals. When I visit England I feel as if I had wandered into the Balkans of light opera or the Marx Brothers. Everyone is at war, nobody gets hurt.

Diversity ought to be encouraging. But I get the impression that the object of writing poems, in England, is to become eligible to enter a national contest in which one receives points for: (1) kicking another poet in the stomach after he has passed out after a literary party; (2) inventing a nasty term which four reviewers plagiarize within eighteen days; (3) going on a reading tour of the United States; (4) acquiring a reputation for extreme cruelty such as to strike terror into the hearts of aspirant poets; (5) publishing twelve books a year; (6) never publishing at all.

In the United States, there is a spirit of *détente*, and people speak to each other who refused to know each other's names a decade ago. For the most part people meet and gossip and argue, and even translate together, who are supposed to oppose each other. I find it useful that Gary Snyder and Galway Kinnell talk about 'biestings'. At a farmer's bar west of Grand Rapids, two miles from the college that gathered everybody, Ted Berrigan and Robert Creeley are shooting pool. John Logan is drinking martinis. Philip Whalen and I talk poetry. Bly is coming tomorrow. Everybody talks all night. But some of the poets wear their shirt sleeves down because they are shooting up. One of them will die of cancer in two months and everyone knows it. Another threatens to get a gun and shoot everybody but doesn't. Is it too cosy? Perhaps. Some of the poets are no good. We don't make an issue of it.

Encouragement. Two poets, Snyder and Bly, are making in their poems irrational systems which integrate everything. Intelligence and learning and the dance! Also encouraging: the ambitiousness of Kinnell's *The Book of Nightmares*, trying to bring together everything that has happened to one man; and Adrienne Rich's separate ambition, in her new poems; and the willingness of some writers, like W. D. Snodgrass, like Richard Wilbur, to walk their own ways even when the way is lonely; and the tough-minded conceptualism of Tom Clark; and the moon-clarity of a very young poet, Gregory Orr. Encouraging also, in a commonplace way: the increasingly oral idea of publication.

Discouraging, in a commonplace way: the proliferation of writers' workshops, and of the products of these classrooms downwards and outwards into an industry of writing classes all of which tend to elevate junk into 'professionalism'. But really, this phenomenon is no more threatening to poetry than Rod McKuen is.

Discouraging—and perhaps a reason for the cosiness: the deaths, the suicides, the madness, alcoholism, methedrine, heroin; the swift vanishing of the older generation, Roethke, Jarrell, Berryman, Lowell; the last most discouraging of all—the author of *Lord Weary's Castle* (and nine subsequent good poems) dissipating into the seedy grandiloquence, the self-serving journalism, of *Notebook*.

Notes on Poetry

POEMS ALOUD

People used to argue about where a poem exists: on the page, or in the ear? The answer is neither: the poem exists in the whole body of the person absorbing it, and most particularly in the mouth that holds the intimate sounds touching each other, and in the leg that dances the rhythm. The ear and the eye, listening and reading, are devices for receiving signals that are dispersed throughout the body. The poem happens *out-loud*, even if you are the fortunate reader who can hear the syllables while he reads silently. The poem is its sounds, and its sounds—mouth pleasures, dance pleasures—are the code which allows the mind to slip back into old and poetic ways of thinking: Ways of fantasy, ways of magic, transformation, metaphor, metamorphoses.

In teaching poetry we tend to glorify something we call *meaning*, and this glorification omits the real body of the poem. When I teach, I talk about the poems after

---

"Poems Aloud" appeared as liner notes on an album called *The Pleasures of Poetry* (Spoken Arts).

I read them, and I talk about anything that seems to me to exist in the poem—figures of speech, vision, the history of words, and even meaning. Talking about poems can help to make sure we are all receiving approximately the same messages. But it *can* hinder, if we think that in talking about the poem we somehow solve it or decode it or turn it into an answer in the back of the book. We don't: The poem remains intact whatever we think we have done to it: It smiles faintly, like a stone Buddha, and will not answer our questions except by reciting itself over again.

Sometimes I think that one of the functions of talking about poems, in a classroom, is to rest up after reading them. The poem itself is so intense, so heavy with emotion and experience, that commentary is a relief from that intensity. We cannot live perpetually at that altitude. We must guard ourselves, however, from substituting the commentary for the poem entirely, even inside our heads as we read the poem. The altitude is frightening perhaps, because the poem is the true embodiment of feeling, and our commentary exists behind the thick glass of remove.

This album, then, should help to introduce poetry to new readers, whether in a classroom or in private. The ultimate goal is to help to create a voice in the reader's imagination—an unspoken voice which pronounces the poem in his head as he reads or remembers the poem. For only when the poem is an audible body to the imagination does the poem exist.

McGRATH'S INVECTIVE

Curse and invective are strangely missing from American poetry. Poets save their invective for other poets, in hate mail that causes short circuits in post offices all over the country. After Pound slammed out at Wall Street bankers, what is there? You can find a little in Allen Ginsberg, a little in Robert Bly. But for the most part our poets are public lovers and private haters. We lack public denunciation, like this:

> And these but the stammering simulacra of the Rand
> Corpse wise men—
> Scientists who have lost the good of the intellect,
> mechanico-humanoids
> Antiseptically manufactured by the Faustian humunculus
> process.
> And how they dream in their gelded towers these
> demi-men!
> (Singing of overkill, kriegspiel, singing of blindfold chess—
> Sort of ainaleckshul rasslin matches to sharpen their
> fantasies
> Like a scout knife.)
> Necrophiles.
> Money protectors.

Thomas McGrath shows the way. This passage comes from his best book, the long autobiographical poem, *Letter to an Imaginary Friend*. There are fine poems in his collected shorter poems, *The Movie at the End of the World*. There are also bad ones: there are also many, many poems with wonderful parts and terrible parts. That's the way he is. Anybody who is put off, and runs away, because of the bad lines, is losing out; also, he is a chickenshit who is scared of anything untidy. McGrath belongs to the line of poets who are perfect in their imperfections (as opposed to poets who are imperfect in their perfections, like Housman.) Here is some more:

> Windless city built on decaying granite, loose ends
> Without end or beginning and nothing to tie to, city down
> hill

From the high mania of our nineteenth century destiny—
    what's loose
Rolls there, what's square slides, anything not tied down
Flies in . . .
                kind of petrified shitstorm.
                                        Retractable
Swimming pools.
                Cancer farms.
                                        Whale dung
At the bottom of the American night refugees tourists
    elastic
Watches . . .

That's not all he does. That's not even what he does best. Sometimes he uses images with an extraordinary audacity: "The sea builds instantaneous lace which rots in full motion—" This image is nearly ghastly, nearly a cliché, and nearly hype; but it leaps across the mile-wide chasm, strenuously and without any grace at all, and lands on all six feet, on the other side, having accomplished a prodigy. (When McGrath misses, the drop is at least three miles, and you can hear the scream from the bottom.) Other such lines: "The citizens wrapped like mummies in their coats with poisoned sleep,/The dreamers, crazed, in their thousands, nailed to a tree of wine. . . "

Actually, what he does best of all is personal reminiscence, like the famous "fuck or fight" story in the first section of *Letter to an Imaginary Friend*.

But other people can tell stories out of their own lives; nobody does invective the way McGrath does it. Here is some more, like my other quotes taken from the second part of *Letter to an Imaginary Friend*:

And to sweep their mountain tops clear of coyotes and
    currency climbers
They have karate-smokers and judy-hypes, the junkies of
    pain,

Cooking up small boys' fantasies of mental muscles, distilling
A magic of gouged eyes, secret holds, charm
Of the high school girls demi-virginity and secret weapon
Of the pudenda pachucas (takes a short hair type
For a long hair joke) power queers; socially-acceptable
   sadists—
Will tear your arm off for a nickel and sell it back for a dime.

I suppose there are twenty people who read the bogus populism of Kenneth Patchen, or the bogus proletarianism of Charles Bukowski, for the one man who reads the real thing, in Thomas McGrath.

THE MULTIPLE PROTAGONIST

In literature much that passes for technique really derives from the structure of the psyche. Critics who are able to discern structure in works of literature—but who know nothing of the emotional life—perpetuate the notion that formal discoveries in literature are gimmicks.

There has never been a formal innovation in writing which did not represent, in the outer and conscious world of language, a shape of the inner and unconscious and wordless process.

A great innovation in modernist English and American literature was the multiple protagonist. The way *The Waste Land* has one character and one character only but that character changes his sex, his name, his history. He is Tireseus, Fisher King, a woman in a pub, a Roman, and Everyman, and Noman, and Emperor,

---

This note on poetry, like most of those that follow, is extracted from a column called "Knock Knock" which appeared in the *American Poetry Review*.

and masochistic cuckold. Eliot virtually copied the shape from Joyce.

The multiple protagonist is a psychic fact not a literary device. Not only are we aware, most intimately in dreams, of our own multiplicity—I am not a person, I am running a boarding house—but in our emotional lives, if there is any deep commitment to another person, *the other person always becomes a cast of characters*. If you love a woman she is daughter, mother, wife, sibling, death's head, and valley grass.

Robert Bly wrote a moderately famous poem called "Counting the Small Boned Bodies." It is a strange and compelling poem. It is "about" the Vietnam war. Many people who have liked it have considered that they were reading a poem about the war, and responding in their feelings to matters connected with the war.

The power of the poem has nothing to do with the war at all. I like the poem very much. The poem is representative of the Giant-Mouse fantasy. The infant has tremendous concerns about scale and size. He invents giants, building them out of the ogres who lean over his crib. He imagines that he is huge and turns the giants into mice. Or he is a mouse, powerful in his ability to hide, but living always in terror of the huge boot.

The fantasy of making bodies smaller is the same as the fantasy of making bodies larger. It is a fantasy of total power, and probably also represents an idealized state of total change, perhaps from the memory of birth. (Alice.) So if it is a power poem, we come back to the war. But only after we have made the journey to infancy.

The poetry of fantasy which is *serious* is poetry which recalls a psychic event of considerable disturbance, as if one put the well down deep enough, not just to get water, but to start the rocks moving under the ground.

WAVING THE DEAD WAND

He had been working in the library for five years. It was hot in there, and stuffy. Finally he walked outside, into the forest.

In a clearing he saw the magician. The old man, who was wearing the skins of animals, waved a wand over a log and it turned into a wolf. Then he waved the wand over a bundle of dried leaves. The leaves rose as children and danced, and ran off into the bushes. Then the magician put his wand down on a tree stump and wandered away.

He crept forward, stole the wand, and ran back to the library with it.

All day, he waves the wand among the shelves of books. In his own eyes, the books are singing. The books discover the North Pole. The books circumnavigate the equator in thirty-two seconds.

I can see nothing but the rows of books.

Or, as Robert Creeley more or less said: Ritual removed from its place of origin says nothing.

POUND'S DEATH

The last of the old ones is dead. I did an interview with Ezra Pound in Rome in 1960. He was hovering at the edge of his decade of silence, but he had not quite entered it. He would begin a complicated sentence one day, pick it up after the semicolon two days later, and ride it home in periodic triumph. He asked me to put the parts together and I did. "Don't let me look so tired," he said.

The obituaries all dealt with the politics, and the "moral dilemma" of the poet-as-fascist. Crap. I don't mean that we must always separate politics from poetics. I mean crap in the case of Ezra Pound. This dilemma is as moral as a broken knee cap; Pound's politics were chemical.

By the early thirties—when he sounded like a simple-minded populist in his attacks on Wall Street—he confided to visitors in Rapallo that the bankers had sent spies to watch every move he made.

Paranoia is *not* a moral matter. It is not dramatic. It is not even interesting. To distort Pound's life into a confrontation between ethics and aesthetics is to be sentimental, and to ignore the real distortions of his disease.

Praise the poetry, lament the lunacy, and get on with it.

THE CRIMSON-HUED CONVEYANCE

I just spent five weeks in England. I love the country, and I could not live there. My speech goes crazy. After seventy-two hours there, I say (of a proposed journey): "It will be difficult to obtain a conveyance." My wife understands; I mean that it will be hard to get a taxi.

English poets don't have to write like this. (Some do.) I pick up this precise polysyllabic argot—just as a newcomer to the United States may collect low idioms until he sounds like a slang dictionary. If I lived in England I would rewrite Williams's wheelbarrow:

> Such an extraordinary degree of importance
> is attached
>
> to a crimson-hued conveyance
> for waste material
>
> which has accumulated particles of liquid
> emanating from the heavens
>
> in the approximate vicinity
> of the albino poultry

I think I'll stay here.

CONCEPTUAL POETRY

Yoko Ono lines up a series of empty flower pots, with the title, "Imagining Flowers." This is conceptual art, very cool, very intellectual, you do the work.

The East Village/Bolinas kibbutz has many rooms. It has lists, it has Pepsi, friendship, and Daily Life. But maybe the most important thing it does sometimes is conceptual poetry.

Aram Saroyan is author of the only poem I know about in the *Guinness Book of Records*. It's there as the world's record shortest poem. It's his famous work,

> blod

which every one knows by heart. It's minimal, and I think it's conceptual, as is work by the Englishman

Tom Raworth, some of Ron Padgett, a little of Ted Berrigan but not Berrigan's best—and most recent work by Tom Clark.

This is what will happen after the *untergang* of irrationalism. It's a Dada rationalism, highly intelligent, using intelligence not for the promulgation of ideas but for the manipulation of the syntax of the medium. When "feeling" occurs, it is camped into sentimentality, and made funny.

One of the most obvious features of conceptual poetry—in reaction to expressionism, surrealism, and romanticism in general—is a strong and committed contempt for emotion.

POEMS ALOUD AGAIN

Poets read poems better than actors. All poets know this. Actors disagree.

Poets read poetry better than actors because they pay no attention to what the poems mean. Because they know that "meaning" is more complicated than some damned explication or interpretation. The actor, trained on the conventional stage, looks for "the motivation of the speaker." (The actor sounds like an English teacher.) When he finds it, he *characterizes* the speaker of the poem by the voice he uses.

The poets speak the voice of the poem, which is the voice of the noise, all the wild inward stuff of sounds. The noise comes from the mouth and is heard by the mouth, and from the listening mouth it travels directly to the bowels and the genitals.

Vowels do this mostly, and resemble the volume in

sculpture. Consonants are more intellectual, travel to the eye, and resemble painting.

POETS' READING

Poets can read their contemporaries for confirmation or for contradiction.

Some good poets don't read their contemporaries at all. They read mystics or Marxists, anthropology or ecclesiastical history—but never poetry. Others read old poetry, or poetry in a foreign language, but never their contemporaries. Some avoid contemporaries because they feel contempt for them. Others are afraid that they will pick up the manners of anybody they admire. Enthusiasm always leads to ventriloquism. Yet another sort of poet *never* sounds like the poets he has been reading, even when he wants to. When he tries to write parody or pastiche, he fails ignominiously; he always sounds weirdly himself, like someone who cannot shake an accent.

For better or worse, many poets read poetry incessantly: for pleasure, for spite, to see what's happening, and to guess what will happen next.

Poets can read either for confirmation (finding and liking poems which resemble their own, in ambition, scope, and tone) or for contradiction (finding poems alien to their own, founded in wholly different wishes for poetry—but which they like anyway). Confirmation is useful when a poet is feeling his way toward a kind of poem that is new to him. Most of the time, contradiction is more useful still.

The trouble with reading for contradiction is that

your taste is likely to be bad. It is easier to judge when you read the kind of poem you know about from trying to make it. Reading for contradiction, you can fool yourself into admiring something because it is your own opposite.

But reading for contradiction, you open yourself to the possibilities of dialectic. And the dialectic keeps you moving, and moving is what you have to do.

GINSBERG OLDER

Allen Ginsberg's new book is beautiful, the best of his books.

So it is not true that men must dissipate and decay as they grow older, lose energy and slacken and despair.

Ginsberg is more lyrical, more mellow, more warm than he ever was. I went back to *Howl* to make sure. It stays where it was, electric and imperative, but *The Fall of America* is better poetry; images instead of rhetoric. Shrill power gives way to quieter and more confident open song:

> Western Air boat bouncing
> under rainclouds stippled
> down grey Rockies
> Springtime dusk,
> Look out on Denver, Allen,
> mourn Neal no more,
> Old ghost bone loves departed
> New lives whelm the plains, rains
> wash Rocky mountainsides
> World turns under sun eye
> Man flies a moment Cheyenne's
> dry upland highways
> A tiny fossil brachiopod in pocket

Precambrian limestone clam
fingernail small
four hundred fifty million years old

These poems include everything. They have the openness, and the associationism, of the *Cantos*, without the spasmodic coherence, and without Pound's sweetness of speech; nobody, not even Keats, has that sweetness. But Ginsberg includes more emotional experience than Pound does, and his energy is compassionate like Whitman's, and he shows spiritual endurance and adventurousness as well as the energy of tender observation. Radio talk, news, city and country, politics, despair, highways and airports, sex, bits of conversation, ideas, sounds, transcendence, tastes, elegies for Cassady and Kerouac—all together. Reading them, you enter the universe of a man's life, as you do with Tom McGrath's *Letter to an Imaginary Friend*.

These poems come out of Ginsberg's notebook, that he keeps in his pocket, and writes in every day. After years, he goes back to his notebooks, and he prints what remains vital. Then we can carry it in our pockets. Vital signs.

THE DAVID HALL COLLECTION

There are people who use the vanity and hopes of people to cheat them or to manipulate them to perform some service. There are the vanity presses, which print books by people who can't print them otherwise, and the vanity anthologies, which charge you for printing your poem. There are also operations which play upon the vanity of published writers. I suppose the universities, and their libraries, have been the worst exploiters of all. But sometimes they go about it *blatantly*.

In my mailbox a few years ago I found this letter, on the letterhead of the University Library of Boston University:

Mr. David Hall
1715 South University
Ann Arbor, Michigan

Dear Mr. Hall:

I am sure that many institutions have been in contact with you asking that they might become the repository of your manuscripts and correspondence files. I write to say that Boston University would be honored to establish a David Hall Collection, and to plead our particular cause for these reasons.

We are in the midst of planning the building of a magnificent new library on our Charles River Campus and we hope to make this library a center of study and research in contemporary literature. Up to the present time Boston University has been growing so rapidly as a "national" institution, that we have waited until we were ready with the proper facilities before establishing such a literary research center. With the advent of our new building we are now ready to embark upon this project.

It is our hope to collect the papers of outstanding contemporary literary figures, house and curate these materials under the optimum archival conditions, and attract to us scholars in the field of contemporary literature who would utilize our institution as a research base.

A David Hall Collection would certainly be a distinguished nucleus around which this University could build a great literary center. Your papers would be preserved for future generations. I do hope that you will look sympathetically upon our request. May I say personally how much I have enjoyed your published work.

Sincerely yours,

Howard B. Gotlieb
Chief of Reference and
Special Collections.
Boston University Libraries

HBG:aw

At first I glanced at the letter carelessly, and found it similar to a letter I had received from another library a few months earlier; I had lost the earlier letter and never answered it. I knew the librarian's game: solicit the works of four-hundred contemporary writers, offering flattery and no cash; fifty years later if the net has caught William Faulkner and Wallace Stevens, you can cheerfully discard the other three-hundred and ninety-eight.

Then I noticed that Mr. Gotlieb, in the extremities of his personal admiration for me, had mistaken my name. Considering the tone of the letter, I thought the mistake hilarious. I delighted in Mr. Gotlieb's prospective embarrassment. I wrote him:

Thank you for your letter of December 14th, which contains sentences like, "A David Hall Collection would certainly be a distinguished nucleus around which this University could build a great literary center." It is very flattering indeed. Flattering to David Hall, that is. Actually there is no one of that name at this address, but I will keep your letter and give it to him when I meet him, so that he can read your tribute to his published work, which you have enjoyed so much.

I wondered how he would excuse himself. Here is what he wrote me:

> I have been shattered by your letter of December 20, and you indeed have every reason to be justifiably angry about the error in your name in my previous letter.
>
> There is really no excuse that I can offer, for it is solely my fault. I dictate my letters and when my secretary puts them on my desk for signature, I sign without reading. I have been spoiled over the years by an excellent secretary, and have thus never proofed my letters once typed. But I have learned my lesson, for when my long-time secretary finally made a typing or transcribing error, it was a whopper.
>
> I offer you my apologies, and only hope that you will accept them.

A gracious letter, a sincere apology. I felt mean.

Then I looked back at the original letter. "David" occurred at the top of the letter, and twice during the text. If he had really dictated the letter, could he have dictated "Donald" three times, and his secretary transcribed "David" each time? Also I noticed that the letter was amazingly general. Full of praise as it was, and personal enjoyment, it could have been addressed to an essayist, novelist, cookbook-writer or whatever, as well as to David or Donald Hall. I began to suspect a form letter, and some sort of verbal order: "Miss Worthington, send out the B401 letter to W. S. Merwin, Sandra Hochman, James Wright, Donald Hall, and Gene Baro. We're running low on poets."

At about this time, by coincidence, an English friend who writes novels wrote me that he had received a most flattering letter from Boston University: did I think he could get any money out of them? I advised him to ask for it, and enclosed a xerox of the David Hall letter. (I also sent a xerox to Robert Bly in Paris; I knew he would think it was funny.) The novelist answered that my letter and his were identical, except that Mr. Gotlieb's secretary got his name right. Then Carol Bly sent me this passage from the *Saint Magazine*, from a column in which the author of the Saint stories, Mr. Leslie Charteris, writes about odds and ends:

> *Undoubtedly the most flattering letter of the year, if not of my whole life, came on the letterhead of Boston University, and read as follows:*

Dear Mr. Charteris:

I am sure that many institutions have been in contact with you asking that they might become the repository of your manuscripts and correspondence files. I write to say that Boston University would be honored to establish a Leslie Charteris Collection, and to plead our particular cause for these reasons.

We are in the midst of planning the building of a magnificent new library on our Charles River Campus and we hope to make this library a center of study and research in contemporary literature. Up to the present time Boston University has been growing so rapidly as a "national" institution, that we have waited until we were ready with the proper facilities before establishing such a literary research center. With the advent of our new building we are now ready to embark upon this project.

It is our hope to collect the papers of outstanding contemporary figures, house and curate these materials under the optimum archival conditions, and attract to us scholars in the field of contemporary literature who would utilize our institution as a research base.

A Leslie Charteris Collection would certainly be a distinguished nucleus around which this University could build a great literary center. Your papers would be preserved for future generations. I do hope that you will look sympathetically upon our request. May I say personally how much I have enjoyed your published work.

Sincerely yours,

Howard B. Gotlieb
Chief of Reference and
Special Collections.
Boston University Libraries

Mr. Charteris agreed to the suggestion, and received further letters from Mr. Gotlieb:

We were of course delighted to receive your letter of May 18, and are honored that this University will be the repository of your papers and thus able to preserve the record of your distinguished career.

That practically all of your writing over the past years was done on the typewriter by no means lessens the value of your "manuscripts." The typescripts will be of literary value since they represent your technique and the body of your work. So please throw nothing else away since we wish our Leslie Charteris Collection to be as complete as possible. (Think how your future biographers will bless us.)

After I sent him a first few (to me) miserable sample items, he wrote again:

Many thanks for your letter of November 13, I am pleased to know of your current plans.

The two articles on you and on the Saint in the Fleetway *Record* were most interesting, and filled me in on many details which, as curator of the Leslie Charteris Collection, I should know. Please do save such notes on your criticism of television scripts as those you sent me. These should be a part of the Collection as should copies of your letters incorporating these ideas.

As I wrote before, we wish the Leslie Charteris Collection to be as complete a record as possible of your life and career. In other words, every letter, every note, every manuscript, every typescript, every clipping you ever saved. Several months ago several of our book dealers started a search to fill in our Charteris holdings as we are attempting to secure a copy of everything you have published in all forms. We have been quite successful to-date, and the materials are slowly coming in.

It will be a great research Collection some day for your future biographers.

I am now busily shipping to Boston what would have formerly become the contents of my wastebasket.

My suspicions, you might say, were confirmed. I hadn't answered Mr. Gotlieb's apologies addressed to my justifiable anger, and I was beginning to phrase a reply when suddenly I had another from him. It began "I enclose a letter I have received from one Robert Bly." Here is the enclosure, Bly's letter to Gotlieb:

I understand that you are interested in beginning a David Hall Collection. This is an encouraging sign, particularly with the good archival conditions there. There are several writers over here whom you might write to for manuscripts, for example, the novelist James Paul Sartre. There is a younger man here also who writes a lot of letters, Francis Sagan.

I found Bly's letter funny, but Mr. Gotlieb did not. Here is his letter to me:

I enclose a letter I have received from one Robert Bly,

concerning my initial request for your papers. Since in my letter to you of December 23rd I tried to very carefully explain how the most unforgivable error in your name occurred, I consider Mr. Bly's letter somewhat intemperate, and quite frankly rude.

At any rate, I thought that you might like to have it.

In his anger, Mr. Gotlieb achieved the true flavor of dictation; calling Bly's letter "somewhat intemperate" and "frankly rude" is like saying that the weather is "rather warm" and "damned hot." At this point I wrote him a letter which he never answered, but which I trust he saved for my future biographers. I accused him, in effect, of exploitation by sycophancy. The profession of writing is insecure and ill-paid. Manuscripts are worth money. Writers who simply mail their manuscripts to Mr. Gotlieb are giving away property, in return for the flattery of a form letter.

But maybe, after all, that's just what they want. Money isn't everything—as writers often tell us—and I suspect that many of them make less from their writing than Mr. Gotlieb makes from collecting their manuscripts. Writers daydream about fame more than they do about riches. Whenever the telephone rings, it's always the King of Sweden: "The Nobel Prize Committee has asked me to inform you . . . " Knowing this weakness, an intelligent manipulator is able to use it for his own ends. Mr. Gotlieb may not be the King of Sweden, but he is as close to the King of Sweden as most of us are likely to get.

Robert Lowell

Some modern artists, like Piet Mondrian or Franz Kline, have exploited a personal calligraphy throughout their artistic lives. But the greatest modern artists, typically, have innovated ceaselessly, moving from style to style and continually destroying their old solutions in search of new matter and manner. The latter sort of artist, as inventive as Edison, includes Picasso and Stravinsky; in literature, Yeats, Joyce, Pound, and Roethke.

While the degree of Robert Lowell's achievement is difficult to assess at this time, he clearly belongs among the changing innovators of modern art. In his thirty years of publishing, he has confounded his admirers by renouncing an achieved style and exploring new territory. Because of his dissatisfaction with his achievement and because that achievement has already been considerable, he has the potential to become the major poet in English of the last half of this century, as Yeats—who recurrently judged himself a failure, and set out to improve his art—was the major poet of the first half.

Lowell has had to resist the temptation to become a monument; it is a temptation actively offered: the literary entrepreneurs of the academy and the press would like to cast him in bronze as The Genius of Contemporary Poetry, so that they could stop thinking about poetry. Lowell's strength has been his obdurate commitment to artistic excellence. Monuments do not write poems. It is up to him, whether in fifty years he looks as Yeats looks to us now, or whether he more closely resembles another intelligent innovator, but a man of less achievement, the laureate Robert Bridges.

Lowell's first collection was a small edition of *The Land of Unlikeness* in 1944. The best of these poems were revised and reprinted in *Lord Weary's Castle* in 1946; the years at the end of the war were astonishingly productive. The petulance and melodrama of much of *The Land of Unlikeness* disappeared; *Lord Weary's Castle* was simply the most powerful book of poems written in our language since *The Tower*. The poems were formal, a tight decasyllable always rhymed; yet the violent energy of the diction—especially embodied in a series of monosyllabic verbs which were frequently tactile—hammered against the decasyllabic cage. Enjambment was violent, caesura eccentric, and the din deafening. Subject matter was painful conflict, particularly within the confines of a rigorous Catholicism to which Lowell brought a strong element of New England Calvinism. Pain, tight form, energetic diction and syntax all combine in this passage from "New Year's Day":

> In the snow
> The kitten heaved its hindlegs, as if fouled,
> And died. We bent it in a Christmas box
> And scattered blazing weeds to scare the crow
> Until the snake-tailed sea-winds coughed and howled
> For alms outside the church whose double locks
> Wait for St. Peter. . . .

This poem is medial in its violence, for *Lord Weary's Castle* varies from an extreme which is close to the spitting jerkiness of the poems left behind in *Land of Unlikeness*, nearly too angry or painful for coherent speech, to the relatively smooth narrative couplet of later poems like "After the Surprising Conversions" and "Between the Porch and the Altar." The celebrated "Quaker Graveyard at Nantucket" is medial also, but leans toward the earlier, more violent style. The later narrative poems include character and start Lowell toward the inclusiveness which he has always envied in the novel. The prosody and diction diminish in violence, and resemble the model that Lowell himself has named, the Robert Browning of "My Last Duchess" and of "Sordello." Perhaps the best of the dramatic monologues belongs to Lowell's second major book, *The Mills of the Kavanaughs*, the magnificent "Mother Marie Therese":

> The bell-buoy, whom she called the Cardinal,
> Dances upon her. If she hears at all,
> She only hears it tolling to the shore,
> Where our frost-bitten sisters know the roar
> Of water, inching, always on the move
> For virgins, when they wish the times were love,
> And their hysterical hosannas rouse
> The loveless harems of the buck ruffed grouse,
> Who drums, untroubled now, beside the sea—
> As if he found our stern virginity
> *Contra naturam. . . .*

The style and manner are perfectly achieved; one could imagine the poet spending the rest of his life comfortably in this decasyllabic rocking chair. But the modern artist is typically unable or unwilling to work within the limits of his known abilities. In the title poem of this volume, Lowell failed. Lyric obscurity and ellipsis prevented his narrative. For several years, Lowell printed virtually nothing; eight years elapsed before the next volume, *Life Studies*.

The new book was a thorough departure. It was auto-biographical, it was largely free verse, and the American edition included prose. Instead of noble thunder out of Virgil and Calvin, one read, "Tamed by Miltown, we lie on mother's bed." In the decade of the fifties, Lowell had gone through enormous changes in his personal life; he was divorced, he left the Catholic church, he experienced the first of the attacks of madness which have committed him to mental hospitals on several occasions, he was remarried, and he became a father. His attitude toward his old poetry shifted; in conversation he told friends that his old poetry seemed melodramatic, posturing. And modern poetry, in general, he felt, was inferior to the modern novel because it excluded so much of reality. Psychotherapists turned him more directly to examining his own experience, in particular his childhood; one started him on a prose autobiography, which became the excellent "91 Revere Street," which was included in the American *Life Studies*. The poet W. D. Snodgrass was a student of Lowell's at Iowa, and began to write poems out of his own life, in a manner which has been called confessional; Lowell observed the possibility, and has acknowledged his indebtedness. Yet another source of his change (and there are doubtless more to be found) was the vogue of poetry reading; in America the enormous popularity of the poetry reading has conditioned American poets to the sound of their own poems in their own mouths. The vogue did not begin until after *Lord Weary's Castle*. Reading his old poems aloud to audiences, Lowell found himself wanting to relax them, to make them more like speech. In this source of change he resembled Yeats, whose poems became more speech-like when he found himself writing for the stage; contact between voice and audience showed up poetic diction of early work, for both men.

Whatever the sources, *Life Studies* was a superb book. There are echoes of earlier Lowell, even to intact iambic pentameters, but the voice is usually quieter and more intimate, as in this passage from "Skunk Hour":

> One dark night,
> my Tudor Ford climbed the hill's skull;
> I watched for love-cars. Lights turned down,
> they lay together, hull to hull,
> where the graveyard shelves on the town. . . .
> My mind's not right.

Lowell's readers tended to argue the merits of the disparate styles, without seeming able to encompass the whole man. But Lowell was to confound them further. In 1961 he brought out *Imitations*, a collection of translations which are largely inaccurate on purpose, adaptations which either attempt obliquely to express the feeling of the original or frankly to use the translated images to make new Lowell poems. As with Ezra Pound's translations, many of which could be called imitations, Lowell's readers are allowed in this volume to observe a part of the education of a major poet: his assimilation—which sometimes includes distortion—of his sources.

In 1964-65 Lowell published two books. *For the Union Dead* carried on the styles of *Life Studies*, with especial success in the title poem, but with energy that frequently reminds us of *Lord Weary's Castle*. In *The Old Glory*, Lowell collected his first attempts at theater (he has also been translating—or imitating—plays; his *Phaedra* has been produced on several occasions). The plays ran successfully in New York, and *Benito Cereno* had good notices in particular. In 1967 Lowell published a brief collection of poems and imitations called *Near the Ocean*. Along with *The Mills of the Kavanaughs*, it is among his lesser work. The imitations are of quality, but the seven original poems, largely written in an elliptical neoclassic tetrameter couplet, fail to make a new resting place for the poet. They seem to thresh and founder within received or achieved moods of diction, not necessarily Lowell's. They seem dissatisfied with their own definition. They remind one of the earlier failures. After *The Land of Unlikeness* came *Lord Weary's Castle*, after *The Mills of the Kavanaughs*, *Life Studies*.

Yet after *Near the Ocean* came *Notebook 1967-1968*, in 1969. It is another failure, grander in its scope and more abysmal in its sinking. The line is generally iambic, and at first glance seems a return to the high bravado of *Lord Weary*; but really the rhythm is slack, and the meter metronomic. The series of unrhymed fourteen-liners imitates John Berryman's *Dream Songs* in ellipses and in subject matter. Lowell writes topical poems—on assassinations and political campaigns—as if he were striving to become known as the conscience of his times; these verses read like prayers to Stockholm. One looks back to *Lord Weary's Castle* and *Life Studies* for confirmation; yes, he made great poems. Perhaps he will make them again.

Or perhaps he will simply rewrite *Notebook* over and over again, for the rest of his life, like an old actor constantly making farewell appearances. In 1970 he published *Notebook*, in which, as he wrote, "about a hundred of the old poems have been changed, some noticeably. More than 90 new poems have been added." In 1973, *Notebook* divided into two, and spawned a third collection. *History* included most of the *Notebook* poems, revised, and added 80 new poems. *For Lizzie and Harriet* reprinted from *Notebook* the 60-odd poems about Lowell's former wife and his daughter, "In another order, in other versions. . . ." The third 1973 book was *The Dolphin*, more than 100 further exercises in the form—14 lines, still mostly unrhymed, frequently iambic—which has dogged the poet for six years. One of the new *History* poems talks about opening "an old closet door," to find "myself/covered with quick-lime, my face deliquescent . . . /by oversight still recognizeable . . .":

> Ah the swift vanishing of my older
> generation—the deaths, suicide, madness
> of Roethke, Berryman, Jarrell and Lowell,
> "the last the most discouraging of all
> surviving to dissipate *Lord Weary's Castle*
> and nine subsequent useful poems
> in the seedy grandiloquence of *Notebook*."

Lowell quotes (and rewrites; the critic said "good" not "useful") an unnamed critic, who spoke not only of "the seedy grandiloquence" of *Notebook*, but of its "self-serving journalism." Reading these latest versions, a reader might find the poems more "self-exploiting" than "self-serving." One senses the life lived in order to provide material for poems; one sees the cannibal-poet who dines off portions of his own body. And the bodies of his family. The verse remains strangely lacking in sensuality, monotonously heavy, sensational, and dishonest.

An Interview

With Gregory Fitz Gerald and Rodney Parshall

The Man in the Dead Machine

High on a slope in New Guinea
the Grumman Hellcat
lodges among bright vines
as thick as arms. In 1942,
the clenched hand of a pilot
glided it here
where no one has ever been.

In the cockpit the helmeted
skeleton sits
upright, held
by dry sinews at neck
and shoulder, and webbing
that straps the pelvic cross
to the cracked
leather of the seat, and the breastbone
to the canvas cover
of the parachute.

Or say that the shrapnel
missed him, he flew
back to the carrier, and every
morning takes his chair, his pale
hands on the black arms, and sits

This videotaped interview began with the reading of a poem.

upright, held
by the firm webbing.

*"The Man in the Dead Machine" has a speculative cast
to it, almost a fantasy quality. Tell us what made you
choose such a subject for your poem.*

The subject matter chooses *you*, really. I can tell you
how it began. I was driving along the New York Thru-
way, alone. Suddenly I had an intense visual image.
Most of my poems begin with language, with words,
rhythm. But this one began with a really strong vision. I
had the vision of a crashed airplane; well, not really
crashed, landed pretty intact, in a jungle, with vines
growing all around it and a skeleton upright in the cock-
pit. I pulled over to the side of the road, illegally (unless
a poem is an emergency, which for a poet it is). I pulled
over and wrote down a prose paragraph describing what
I'd just seen. I recognized that it was an image of how I
felt in my life, then. It wasn't a good patch. I didn't do
much about the image for many months. Perhaps a year
afterward I began to work on it. I began with the intro-
duction and then the description of the skeleton, which
was the strongest thing. Then I wanted to bring him
back into the contemporary world, to say that it made
no matter whether he was dead or alive. I had all sorts
of terrible ideas, like calling it his identical twin, who
was wandering around in New York City. I couldn't get
it right. Until finally, I saw again what you can do in
poetry: use the possibility of fantasy, of dreams. Or say,
"Suppose I was lying?" Why not say that? It makes no
difference.

I had other problems in writing it. For instance, when
it first came out in a magazine, it didn't read "his pale/
hands on the black arms," it read "every/morning takes
the train, his pale/hands on the black case." I like the

assonance there, with "case," and "train," and "pale." I like the sound of it. But it came to me that it looked like another poet attacking the businessmen, another poet attacking the commuters. Well, I can do that if I want to, but that's not what I wanted to do, this time, at all. I wanted to implicate *everybody*: me, you, *everybody*, in this sense of being "the man in the dead machine." I didn't want to limit it to a social class.

That suggests that "The Man in the Dead Machine" is apolitical. But what do you think about poets who write so much on political subjects, let's say about the Indo-China War?

I don't have any general feeling. I think some of Robert Bly's work, which includes the Vietnam war, is fantastically good—"The Teeth Mother Naked at Last," the long poem, is terrific, and so are some of the shorter ones. But poems are never *about* anything. I mean, what's "The Man in the Dead Machine" about? Is it about the middle-aged man, the Second World War? I don't know what it's about except that it embodies a feeling. It's pretty much a single feeling, but not entirely. The spider web is never mentioned in that poem, but the skeleton is like a fly in a web, a spider's web; webbing is mentioned, but not a spider's web, and then there are those vines like arms: I think of the mother embrace—that embrace is death also. The mother spider.

In order to write with the Vietnam war as part of your subject, or as an ostensible subject, or a beginning to it, the event has to touch something in your own life, your inner life, very strongly. For instance, when someone asked him, "Are you a pacifist?" Sigmund Freud answered, "No, I'm not aggressive enough." Now in order to write out of the misery and horror of the Vietnam war, you have to have a lot of murder in you. If you want to write out of indignation, go write an editorial, go run a political campaign—that's great—but indignation is not going to make poetry. Poetry has to come out of something in you, part of which was there even when you were two or three years old.

Does that explain Bly's "Small Boned Bodies"?

Yes. That's a poem of intense fantasy, the fantasy of making things tinier or larger, like Alice in Wonderland. It's one of the characteristics of the infantile mind, the ability to change the size of things. It comes about probably because the baby is so aware of disparities: his own smallness against the hugeness of the giants that hover over him.

Does that suggest that poets have child-like minds?

Poets are people who have to be in touch with that part of themselves. There's power in that kind of thinking—the prerational thinking, as opposed to the kind of thinking that begins about ten, eleven, and twelve. Prerational thinking has power for transformation, for understanding; it has the power of dream. There's an incredible source of energy of dream thinking. That's not actually to *be* a child. It is, from time to time, to think like one, to let your mind perform like a child's. Still it's to be a man, a more complete man.

You're talking about an aesthetic for modern poetry, as distinct from earlier poetries. Words that describe the impact of the modern poem like "epiphany" or "transport" or "gut feeling," are taking the place of words like "theme" or "idea." Do you agree?

Yes, but I'm not sure it's a difference in poets; it may be a difference in the critics.

That opens up a whole new bag of beans, doesn't it?

It's a difference in the way we talk *about* poetry, more than it's a difference in the way we write it. I think there's a fantastic continuity in lyric poetry, from the early Greeks to the present. Remember that poem by Robert Graves, "To Juan at the Winter Solstice"? It begins, "There is one story and one story only." Sometimes I think that all poetry is one story. And that story is: transform yourself, release yourself from the control of civilization. That's why Plato had to kick it out of the *Republic*. Plato was absolutely reasonable to do so.

That question of restraint brings up the subject of, let's say, the Beat movement of the 1950s. The Beats decried restraints. Now you edited the Penguin Contemporary American Poetry, *the 1962 edition, and omitted most of the Beat poets. Why did you do that? What was your principle?*

Taste. Partly bad taste and partly good taste. I left out Allen Ginsberg, and I shouldn't have.

He's in the new 1972 edition.

He's in the new edition. There's some of his work that I like a lot; he should have been in there before. Gary Snyder *was* in the original edition. He went up on the mountain with Jack Kerouac, in the *Dharma Bums*, so he's a Beat if there ever was one. But I really don't like the poetry of Lawrence Ferlinghetti; I don't think it's any good. I understand he's a good man, a most generous man. But I don't like his poems.

This implies an aesthetic though, doesn't it? Or is it just taste, a private taste? Or is it a taste you could define in the conventional terms the critic would accept?

No, I can't.

Or that a teacher could utilize?

I utilize it, when I'm a teacher. But the aesthetic is a shifting, constantly moving thing, and I think it shifts and moves to accommodate taste. In the very early fifties, most of us had an aesthetic which prompted us to use words like "tightness" and "hardness." And I certainly believed in the usefulness of rhyme, meter, and so on. I've shifted totally, so that my words are "intense," "original"—more romantic words. But I still want a poem to be resolved. I hear resolution in William Carlos Williams, and in Robert Creeley, as much as I do in Richard Wilbur.

One of your poems, "Reclining Figure," is of this sort.

It's a free verse poem, but what does that mean? It just means that it's free of any arithmetic that anybody ever added up before.

Students sometimes think that free verse is easier to write than more formal kinds of verse. What is your reaction to that?

I think that's naive. You can learn to write iambic so that you write it as fast as your hand can move. You can even talk it. A couple of weeks ago I was in Iowa with Don Justice. He and I started talking iambic back and forth to each other. In fact, we were rhyming it for a while too. That's just a trick. Now, to write good poetry is *not* a trick. But iambic by itself is easy to learn. You put in six months or two years, and it's easy. Then it gets tough, when you want to write a good poem.

The exciting thing to me about free verse is that you don't know where you're going—you have no guidelines. If you're beginning a sonnet, you know a lot about what the ninetieth syllable is going to be like, before you get to it. You have a lot of information; in that sense, the sonnet is redundant. (It's still hard to write a good sonnet, heaven knows.) In free verse there's the adventure of beginning something and not knowing where you're going. Maybe the first line will determine what comes later, but only in retrospect will you know how it did so. There's this wonderful sense of tentative exploration, reaching out, revising, changing, working for what sounds right. When you're writing iambic, you know you have to find, say, a word that is three syllables long with the loud noise on the middle syllable. You've got a lot of information about the word you're looking for. But in free verse you have no idea.

Control, insofar as control exists, is instinctive?

It's based upon years and years of reading poems, loving poems. . . .

It's learning, but not in any formal sense?

It's learning, but only if you don't know what you're looking for. Now I'll read "Reclining Figure":

Reclining Figure

Then the knee of the wave
turned to stone.

By the cliff of her flank
I anchored,

in the darkness of harbors
laid-by.

Now you say that's a free verse poem. But it seems to me to be very tightly written. Is there any contradiction in that?

I don't think there's any contradiction. You know what Frost used to say: there's loose iambic and tight iambic. Well, there's loose free verse and tight free verse, and lots in between. "Reclining Figure" is tight free verse. Later I grew dissatisfied with the tightness of my free verse. I thought I wasn't being adventurous enough, so I began to work in a more asymmetrical free verse—long lines, short lines, and so on. I've even been working in prose lately. I seem to be working on the principle that once I feel I can do something, know how to do it, that then I shouldn't do it anymore. You come to rely on what you know you can do; so you've really got to work on your control by doing something you don't know how to do.

It's tiny, but I worked on "Reclining Figure" for a year or so. First it was ten lines long, then eight, then six. The assonance and consonance, the almost internal rhyme of "flank" and "anchored," and of "*dark*ness" and "*har*bors"—these noises were important to me. There's some play with *n*'s and *r*'s: "Then the knee of the wave/turned to stone"; that's the sonority I wanted. But this is all in retrospect. Afterward you say, "Oh, that's why I did that!" In this poem, the coda, the finale, is just those two heavy beats; "laid-by." That puts it to rest, I think.

One American tradition, I suppose you might call it the Eliot-Pound tradition, suggests difficulty. Poems are supposed to be hard. Students complain about this sort of thing. Popular audiences never took to such poems. You've written an essay called "The Ethic of Clarity" that deals with this point.

"The Ethic of Clarity" is about prose style, not about poems. My idea in that essay was to point out that there's a continuity among modern writers—an attitude toward language. It's prose language I'm talking about. The value of style is to be judged not for its invention, not for its cleverness, not for its rhetoric, but for its *honesty*. And clarity is almost a definition of honesty. Hemingway says it; Pound says it; George Orwell says it. These are very different people. Pound and Hemingway were friends, but obviously they wrote enormously differently. But when they wrote about prose, they were saying the same thing.

As far as poetry goes, there are several kinds of obscurity which are really distinct. The obscurity of reference in Eliot and Pound—the obscurity of learning— is such a totally different thing from, say, the obscurity of not knowing what someone is up to. When Wordsworth's critics accused him of obscurity, the obscurity was obviously of the second kind. His critics weren't used to his style. What was it? It couldn't be poetry!

If somebody finds a poem like my "Reclining Figure" obscure, it's because the poem doesn't tell a story, or have an argument, or have characters in dialogue. The poem doesn't do what you expect it to. It does something else, which the reader is not used to. This kind of obscurity is a sign that the poet may be doing something that hasn't been done frequently in the past; therefore it's a good sign.

By "clarity" you don't mean "simplicity"—the kind of thing that the pop audience can grasp. You mean instead something that's suggested. You have to learn how to read in order to read poetry, to learn what the poet's up to, what a poem is up to.

Clarity does not mean mass popularity. Clarity means not hazing over, fudging over the edges in dishonesty. The opposite of clarity is obfuscation.

Your concern with clarity indicates that you're concerned with craftsmanship. You talk about several versions, for instance, of "Reclining Figure," first ten lines, then eight lines, and finally six lines. This means a lot of revision.

I take from two to four years to finish a poem, usually.

W. D. Snodgrass's practice is similar. It contrasts very sharply with what Jack Kerouac maintained about his "Mexico City Blues," of which he claimed he never revised a single line. What's your reaction to that kind of statement from a poet?

I don't care how anybody writes anything, if I like the poem. But I am extremely suspicious of what anybody says about how he writes a poem. All poets lie about how they write their poems.

But they lie so entertainingly!

Right! They make their lies interesting, and I listen to their lies carefully. I hope you like my lies, too. Allen Ginsberg writes every day in his journal. So Allen says. Then four or five years later he takes out what's still alive, and that's a poem. Now, that's Allen's view of what Allen does, and it's probably close to what Allen does. Yet, I wouldn't be the slightest bit surprised to discover he'd changed some things here and there. If you asked him, maybe he'd admit he did; but when I talk to him, he gives the impression that he just takes it as is.

I write every day, but I don't write something new every day. Ultimately, maybe we're doing the same thing and coming out with the same amount of work. I find myself telling lies a lot in much of the first draft, in second drafts, and in other drafts. Much of the process of rewriting for me is getting the crap out. It's not just sentimental lies, lies about feelings; it's one's ways of intellectually explaining a figure, draining the feeling out of it. I have to watch myself for that. Many of the feelings I write about, we all write about, are scary. You want to avoid saying them sometimes; or you say them and then you take them back by explaining them. Somebody who writes a whole lot and doesn't revise very much—there're several: William Stafford, Richard Eberhart—probably finds moments when he is able to be true right away. By writing an incredible amount, by writing something new every day, you would probably come on such moments. It's not my way. I don't say that my way is better than anybody else's. It's just the way I have come to.

Snodgrass tells us that he has had certain difficulties, that his first drafts seemed to be too dense and that, as he worked toward the ideal of clarity you were talking about, gradually the poem got simpler and simpler, or, more accurately, apparently *simpler.*

I tend to start with ten pages and end up with half a

page, as I clear away the guff. Clarity isn't something I think of when I work on poetry. I think of intensity, honesty, revelation, discovery. Certainly, though, the process of peeling away sharpens what's there. It doesn't clarify it, it sharpens it. But in the sense I was using the word—talking about prose—clarity is something I'm after, because it's the same as revelation. It's being honest; it's being true; it's saying what you feel, getting it down with no apparatus of adjectives or prettiness or whatever to take away from what is really there.

One of my own dangers in writing is my affliction with sonority and mellifluousness. I love noises in the mouth. There are two kinds of sound in poetry. When people say that somebody has "a good ear," they can mean two very distinct things. There's the kind of ear that moves down the page, paragraphing, breaking the sentence against the line. It's the ear of line breaks, whether it's iambic or free verse. That's the dance. That's related to the infant kicking in the crib. The other kind of sound is the mouth sound: all the vowels, some consonants, and so on. A poem can have both types of sound, obviously. Some poets have both, so they balance, but most poets will tend to value one kind of sound over another. I value the mouth sounds—vowels and stuff. So, I may kid myself about sounds in a poem. I try not to. If I can get a string of three or four diphthongs in a row, it drives me wild. If I can go "ai, ai, ai" in a line, it seems to take off and fly. Yet it might not seem so to other people.

You share that concern for sound with some fine poets of the past; Dante, for instance, who took the same delight in it that you speak of.

Keats!

We teachers really don't teach poetry then, do we? What you're talking about is the real essence of impact, call it what you like. Poetry's really quite unteachable, isn't it?

I'm talking about composition. If you're teaching poetry, I don't think you'd be teaching what it is like to write it; you're teaching the object on the page.

It's true that when I teach poetry, I emphasize the *body* of the poem. Everything that the poem has to do with the senses; not the intellect, or the message, very much. The message is always the last thing for me in poetry.

I think that's a fair definition of very modern poetry. There's little concern for the message.

Look, the best poetry in the language is in the *Oxford Book of Nursery Rhymes*. Somebody always asks you what poetry is. I've been dodging that question for years, but I think I know what it is now. In the sense that we can isolate poetry—that we can find in it something not common to other things—poetry is "Baa, baa, baa, black sheep," or "Peas porridge hot." It's *sounds*. There's a compelling rhythm; there's a magical quality to it; it has powers over you; it's spellbinding. Now that doesn't make it better than John Donne's poetry. But John Donne has "Peas porridge hot" in him too. That's why he's a poet. Most of us, teaching Donne, will talk about the way the metaphors hang together; we'll provide a paraphrase; we'll explain what a compass is. That's easier to talk about than to talk about the "Peas porridge hot" part of John Donne.

I infer from what you say that you think a poet teach-

ing has certain advantages over a teacher who is not a poet.

The way I teach is very much as a poet; that's the only way I know how to do it. I learn a lot from critics and from scholars who were not poets, who give me information, especially about older things. Obviously, to read older poems, you need a little history, for God's sake, to know what the words mean. So I learn from people who do not emphasize the kind of thing I emphasize. Anybody who is really going to get into poetry, or teach it for that matter, should have some literary history and some scholarly background. I would also like him to get from me, or somebody like me, an idea of the sensual body of the poem. The body of the poem is terribly important, but I don't think most teachers feel it.

There's so much in poetry that isn't taught, really great poems that are not taught because there's so little to say about them. Take Thomas Hardy.

Hardy is one of the most beautiful poets in the language. There's a poem called "During Wind and Rain," which is a favorite of mine:

During Wind and Rain

They sing their dearest songs—
He, she, all of them—yea,
Treble and tenor and bass,
    And one to play;
With the candles mooning each face . . .
    Ah, no; the years O!
How sick leaves reel down in throngs!

They clear the creeping moss—
Elders and juniors—aye,
Making the pathways neat
    And the garden gay;

And they build a shady seat . . .
      Ah, no; the years, the years;
See, the white storm-birds wing across!

      They are blithely breakfasting all—
      Men and maidens—yea,
      Under the summer tree,
         With a glimpse of the bay,
      While pet fowl come to the knee. . . .
         Ah, no; the years O!
And the rotten rose is ript from the wall.

      They change to a high new house,
      He, she, all of them—aye,
      Clocks and carpets and chairs
         On the lawn all day,
      And brightest things that are theirs. . . .
         Ah, no; the years, the years;
Down their carved names the rain-drop ploughs.

If you try to paraphrase it you can say: "people have lots of fun together, especially in families; but then they get old and die." We learn something we knew already. "During Wind and Rain" says that four times. That sounds like some dumb poem, but it's not. It's a beautiful, a gorgeous poem. To teach it, to try to get it across to students, you can't talk about ideas.

Poe is the same way. When I teach Poe, I often feel frustrated. There's something there I feel, but which I find incommunicable because only the poem can say it. I can't say it.

When we really read poems, the message or idea is only 5 or 10 percent of it. A poem is like an abstract painting or a piece of rock a sculptor has chipped away at a little and changed so that it's become a wholly satisfying shape.

It's the inner body of the poem—this close-up sound and motion, these assonances together—which makes a poem a spell; which takes you back to a primitive part of the mind, where strange reactions take place. Inside the poem there is a second language. Ideas are just the top side of the poem, the top side of language. They're okay, but why are they practically all that ever gets talked about? Ridiculous! The poem has this intense inner life, this second language. The inside, the spiritual life of somebody dead hundreds of years, or somebody living down the block, is talking to you. If we really can read the poem—and by really reading, I mean taking it into your mouth and into the muscles of your legs—if we *read*, we record the expression the poet has—willy nilly, sometimes not knowing what he is doing—imprinted in the shape and motion of the words. In the end, there's an *unspoken* communication. That is poetry.

Edited from a prose transcription of a videotape interview with Donald Hall in April, 1972, sponsored by the Brockport Writers Forum, Department of English, State University College, Brockport, N.Y. 14420. All rights reserved, State University of New York.

Questions from *Agenda*

The editor of *Agenda*, William Cookson, sent me a questionnaire on "American rhythms" which I answered in a letter. I had the confused notion that he would summarize and paraphrase my remarks. Instead, he printed them. I have here prefaced each answer with the question it was meant to answer, and removed a few answers I cannot find questions for. The questionnaire began with a statement of purpose:

The purpose of this questionnaire is to seek practical answers from poets concerning their methods and intentions in the disposition of their poems upon the page. We are not investigating the absolute nature of rhythm so much as the rhythmic intention behind the print. Because of the variety of rhythmic systems, numbers of questions may seem irrelevant to your practice. Please ignore these and treat the questionnaire as a guide; we would prefer a straightforward account of your practice in continuous prose.

Apart from the obvious differences, such as of accent on words like "temporary" and "civilization," do you recognize in your work a distinction between English and American sufficient to entail new systems of rhythm or metre?

I don't believe in intentions. I never believe what poets say as their intentions, including my own. I think that the whole idea of intention is profoundly naive, and I am surprised to see it recurring in this questionnaire. No one knows for sure what he is doing really. One may intend something, indeed, but if one has a minimum of psychic sophistication, one knows that one's intention and one's accomplishment are related to each other in a devious way at best. Therefore I think almost all of these questions are irrelevant to anybody's practice. Believe me, if you get neat and clean answers from anybody, disbelieve everything that is said. I prefer to take up your points as they happen. There is a distinction between English and American rhythm, but it is not possible to define it in terms of any system of meter, and rhythm is nonsystematic, by definition. It is true that English and American poets make different noises. So do many poets from each other. But it is true that there are typical American noises, which an Englishman cannot make, and cannot even hear. This accounts for the obtuseness of most Englishmen to the ear of William Carlos Williams. It may possibly account for the fact that few Americans can stomach the incredible idea that John Betjeman is a poet. It may also account for the fact that many English critics, once they think they have hit upon what is an American kind of noise, can't tell a fake American idiom poem from a real American idiom poem. This is true of that man at Cambridge, named Prynne. It is also true of that man at London University, Mottram.

How conscious are you of rhythmical considerations? Are poems of yours ever triggered off by a purely rhythmic suggestion?

I am extraordinarily conscious of rhythmical considerations, in some sense. That is, I think that the sound of a poem is its spiritual core. Rhythm is of course only a small part of the sound of the poem, but as such it is part of something terribly important.

Yes, poems of mine are sometimes started, or appear to start, with a rhythm, that is to say a beat, or a little dance motion, but this is a rare event. One poem in which it happened was "The Long River."

Is the disposition of your poems on the page affected by visual concerns?

The disposition of my poems upon the page is ever so slightly influenced by visual appearance, but only when the visual appearance can in fact be duplicated by the voice.

I did not use to do this. When I wrote syllabics, in old days, there were sometimes arrangements which were purely visual and could not serve as notation to the voice.

How do you regard the line-end:
  a) as a minute pause inevitably,
  b) as a pause only when punctuated, or
  c) as a pause, any way, but one lengthened by punctuation?

The line end is a minute pause. It is lengthened by punctuation, if there is any. It is on occasion effective in increasing volume, in raising or lowering pitch, and in making a long syllable longer. For this reason, line breaks can even affect assonance.

What sound-effects are you conscious of using or seeking?

I'm particularly conscious of percussiveness and of assonance. Especially of assonance on long vowels or even diphthongs. When my poems get to their most intense, their most rhapsodic, I find frequently that I am in the middle of a rather percussive series of long "eye" sounds. Or "eee" sounds.

Needless to say, this has nothing to do with an intention of any sort.

Do you compose instinctively, for the ear alone, seeking like Lawrence the effect of spontaneous speech?

I disagree with the statements in this question. I don't know what anybody knows about his instinct, or anybody else's, and I should doubt very much that a literary manner of this sort was a matter of instinct. It is purely preconscious, and learned, albeit imperfectly. And what do you know what Lawrence was seeking? You certainly don't know it because of anything he said about what he was seeking.

Does the line-end indicate your rhythmic intention or unit or is it a result of punctuation and sense alone?

The line-end indicates only a melodic unit. If it coincides with the sense, that is its problem. There is no bloody point using lines unless you mean them to be units of noise.

What use do you make of caesuras in your vers libre?

What the hell does this mean? Pause slows down the line. Pause gives you a chance to take a breath. Pause indicates semantic groupings. We all know that.

Do you do anything to obviate the placing of unimportant words at the line-end?

If I place a word at the end of the line it is no longer unimportant.

How do you define for your own purposes "a syllable"? What do you do about the slurring of syllables that occurs in speech?

A syllable is what is conventionally called a syllable. Hypermonosyllable is counted as one syllable. But that is just my practice. The slurring is something which is maddeningly imprecise about syllabics. But then, syllabics are really just a stage on the way from iambics to free verse.

Do you pay any attention to syllable length, or stress, or consonant content?

If you don't pay attention to syllable length, to stress, or to consonants (I take it that paying attention to consonant content is paying attention to consonants?) then you have no ear at all.

How do you distinguish, except typographically, between say, a three-lined stanza of six syllables and a two-line stanza of nine syllables per line?

Since line structure is everything, the distinction between these two things is enormously important. The question seems very uneducated.

How dead is the pentameter? What do you do to re-animate it?

I don't write it myself. Of course it's not dead. It never was alive. It will be used again.

Do you use a modification of, or the traditional Saintsbury type of system?

Saintsbury had no system. Saintsbury did not understand the first thing about English verse. Don't you know this? Have you ever read Saintsbury? He denied that there was any difference between duration, pitch, or volume. The man could not hear. He was totally incompetent when it came to listening to a poem. As in his famous example of listening to a waltz tune, while studying at Merton (or wherever it was), and suddenly grasping the meter of Homer!!

If English poets have been writing in "the traditional Saintsbury system" it might explain a lot about the imbecility of recent English metrical verse.

Do you counterpoint your metre against the normal speech-rhythm or do you attempt a coincidence?

The only sensible thing is to counterpoint it. But as I said above I'm not doing it at all anyway at the moment.

Do you use rhyme of any sort, if so, which and for what purpose?

Direct rhyme. Or consistently indirect rhyme. It is vulgar to mix direct and indirect rhyme. Auden does it. Auden is consistently vulgar and incompetent in versification, despite rumors to the contrary.

Do you pay any attention in your metrical verse to

length as opposed to stress of syllable or to syllable count?

Anybody who can write a decent line pays attention constantly to length of syllable, to pitch, to syllable count, and to stress of syllable, in writing metrical verse or in writing free verse. However, meter in English pays attention only to the relative stress of syllable, combined of course with the count of syllables. Length of syllable is not a metrical factor. It is of course enormously important to the sound of the poem, and therefore to the value of a poem. But then, so is everything else.

Kinnell

A Luminous Receptiveness

When Galway Kinnell puts his feet into old shoes, bought at the Salvation Army, he does not fill them; the shoes fill him. He is possessed by the shoes, as he is possessed by bears and chickens and children. Though the voice of *The Book of Nightmares* is Galway Kinnell's voice, the poet is without *identity*, as in Keats's wonderful passage. Identity comes from the ego. *Some* good poetry comes from identity; bad poetry is cursed by it.

There is the danger of possession without return (and without poetry); connection with the body and the world fades out; everything becomes impalpable. In *The Book of Nightmares*, "Virginia" incurs this loss, "Virginia" who writes "Dear Galway" a letter signed, "Yours, faithless to this life." Though Kinnell has written a book of death, he is faithful to this life, after his fashion. He feels the lure of the vacuum but he returns bringing images. Death is the underside of everything living, and the skull shines beneath the skin; but, equally, there is no death without the image of resurrection. Man is the house that falls, but to the Catholic imagination there is no fall that does not summon the rise again; we see, "by corpse-light, in the opened cadaver/ of hen, the mass of tiny,/unborn eggs . . ." (*Mass* ?) The eggs will remain unborn, " . . . each getting/tinier and

yellower as it reaches back toward/the icy pulp/of what
is . . ." But there were eggs in the dead hen.

> And when I hoisted
> her up among the young pines, a last
> rubbery egg slipping out as I flung her high, didn't it happen
> the dead
> wings creaked open as she soared
> across the arms of the Bear?

The wings made a cross, then.

Crosses are more common than bears, and *The Book of Nightmares* is the last Mediaeval poem, saturated with the Eastern moment of the Church. ("One image crossed the many-headed . . . " in Yeats.) The Church of possession, and neither of possessions nor of possessing others. It is not the Church of intelligence or of information but of intuition, a passive luminous receptiveness. Kinnell shares this quality of mind with the more Protestant Roethke and Whitman. But Kinnell's death is not Whitman's death nor Roethke's death. It is Calvary, continual and unavoidable. Even to mention avoidance is to be foreign to Kinnell's character; is to summon consciousness or ego or intellect. One does not avoid the particles that make the universe; one sets to receive them.

Peter, "apostle of stone," lives in this book, and "the last grails of light." Bones and skeletons, the "witness tree," "blood sacrifice," and "in the graveyard/the lamps start lighting up, one for each of us,/in all the windows/of stone." When the sky-diver falls, he falls crossed "opening his arms into the attitude/of flight"— and Kinnell becomes the modern man in the Mediaeval woodcut—"as he obeys the necessity and falls . . ." But the idea of obedience brings to the scientific news a religious attitude.

The nightmare is the continual fear: maggots in the corrupt flesh; death for the self experienced through the selves of others; death for the simple self in its nakedness; fear of the continual crucifixion and of the possession which is introduced by images of crosses. There is also the joy which death illuminates. "Death is the mother of beauty," said Stevens. Kinnell says, "*the wages/of dying is love*," which puts a considerable reversal upon the motto of another church. Orthodoxy of any kind would not occur to Kinnell; orthodoxy is belief and belief relies on theology; Kinnell's intuitive assemblage takes its materials from a religion but its structure is the flow of experience; which is to say that the structure does not matter; we swim in *The Book of Nightmares* like a sea without shores. (Or we do not read it at all.) But this sea is huge and contains all of Kinnell's life that he can bring to the page.

I am unable to discover a critical word or phrase which would specify and qualify the saturated untheological Church of Kinnell's reception of the other. We accept because Kinnell's transformations compel us, and the hypnosis of his rhythm possesses us. We do not rebel at doctrine because the poem has no doctrinal design on us. We do not enter *The Book of Nightmares*; it fills us up. The loss of ego is the greatest gain; it is *poetry*.

No review will be adequate to the inclusiveness and complexity of this great book.

More Notes on Poetry

SOME IDEAS ABOUT PROSE POEMS

The current fashion for prose poems points out some limitations of free verse—at least, free verse as most of us have been practicing it.

Any form, insofar as we can name it (the ultimate form is unnamable, different in every poem, therefore the same in every poem) associates itself with an area of thought, a type of psychic experience, and a mode of organization. These namable forms (blank verse of various sorts, sonnets, trimeter tercets, long lined syntactical free verse—whatever) become so associated because of the dominance of particular poets who use the form—not because of anything inherent in the form.

The conventional prosody of the moment is short-lined, assymetrical free verse with a tendency toward terminal caesura. This verse form is associated with fantastic and ecstatic modes of thought and feeling. When it carries information, it becomes wholly boring.

Metrical verse can carry information; the more organized the meter, the more easily the line can carry information. That is, the couplet carries information better than blank verse. The *heroic* couplet—with medial caesura, direct rhyme, and end stop—can carry information more easily than the enjambed couplet. In fact, end stopped, decasyllabic, and medially paused blank verse can do it better than loose blank verse.

Prose poems can carry information too. Prose poems can tell stories. Stories are information. Prose poems can do this because they are associated with prose.

What a revolutionary observation.

Still, it seems paradoxical: prose poems resemble metrical poems, more than they resemble free verse, in the kinds of experience that they can deal with. Prose poems can take a variety of detail, can take more syntax, can take more direction and substantiation.

Poets have been straining at the bonds of ecstatic and fantastic poetry, and prose poems have become a way of moving away from the free form which can seem restrictive.

By no means is prose the form of the future. Prose poems—like syllabics which were fashionable fifteen years ago—are a station on the journey. Everything is a station on the journey.

I suspect that our fascination with the paragraph will end quickly, and that we will work instead with a more varied and useful free verse line. This line will be longer, will be enjambed as well as end-stopped, and derives ultimately from Whitman. Galway Kinnell uses such a line, lucid and passionate and flexible, in *The Book of Nightmares*.

THE ACT OF WRITING

To the poet, the pleasure and the value of writing poetry occur in the act of writing.

When the poet is young, he takes pleasure in publication; the pleasure remains when he is older, but it diminishes a thousandfold; it blows away like dandelions. The pleasure of being praised fades less; and at a poetry reading, there are the pleasures of performance and the rewards of applause. I don't need to say that these various pleasures have a counterpart in pain; today I am talking of the pleasures.

All these rewards are nothing compared to the process of writing itself. Failure frustrates, blockage bouleverses; the act of writing—all writing is action-writing— is recompense for whatever miseries occur with impediment.

Writing poems is not like writing an editorial for a newspaper, or collecting a description of how to knit a sweater.

In these latter activities, we search for words to implement an argument or to name an activity already known ("known" either as inferior or incomplete words, or as images like those which encode rote action). Much bad writing (and bad reading) result from the confusion of poetry with the use of words in other connections, as if words remained "the same material."

Writing poems is more like making sculpture than like making speeches. Poems are objects which we manipulate with the fingers of our tongues.

Sculpture is a useful analogy. Either carving or modeling, though these methods are different. Sculpture creates *volume*. Poems have volume as editorials do not. Rodin said that a sculptor must never think of a surface except as the extension of a volume.

Everything pushes up from under, against the taut surface of the word.

When a young poet says that she wants to walk in the field and love the field, without making words about the field—to stand there in happiness, without hearing "How beautiful!" speak itself inside her head—I can understand her battle. Now, she sometimes uses words to keep the world away, the way ancient men waved fire at elephants.

But in the poem the words are not real weapons. Instead, they are like weapons ancient men so carved and decorated that they stopped being weapons and became sculpture. In the act of making a poem, the words for the field do not become the field. They remain words but they become material we walk into and lie down in.

This sense of action-writing seems to me to destroy a distinction commonly made between seekers and makers. Of course there are seekers who make nothing sensual. (A poem is *for the senses* before it can be for anything else.) And of course there are poets wholly unconscious of seeking; but even for these men, poetry is not merely some metier or craft, like accounting or telegraphy; because a poem (seekers' poems also) is *never about anything*.

The poem is the monument of its moment; it is the surface presenting (present-ing) the volume which is the whole life lived, the psyche's farming harvested, and the history of the race.

Such a complexity is far too multiple to be managed by the consciousness. Only the unacknowledged intelligence can handle so many things at once, and only at certain inexplicable moments can the vast system of the synapses provide metaphor and sound. This is the moment's action which is writing, and it is the moment of the pleasure and the value and the reward.

There are the moments of assemblage, moments when you feel so good that you want to live for a thousand years. They happen when the present and the past fuse in a sudden imagination, and the real Troy becomes visible as the layered wholeness: only the all is the one. This is the formal principle of the poem. Memory flared into the senses of the moment makes the poem. And the boy who walks down the street, in 1942, is the man of this moment, who is forty-four years old.

THE BIGGEST SMALL PRESS

Maybe the biggest small press in history is the Broadside Press in Detroit. Broadside has sold more than 100,000 books by *one* of its young poets. Yet most bookstores, even bookstores which sell poetry, stock no Broadside books. It's invisible; it's black.

Most of the sales have come from black bookstores, like Vaughan's in Detroit, and Don L. Lee (the poet of more than 100,000 copies) is famous mostly within the black world. The publisher and editor is Dudley Randall, who began with broadsides only, and grew into book publishing largely by default. An anthology called *For Malcolm* began his publishing. Now he publishes poetry by Etheridge Knight, Sonia Sanchez, James Randall, Nikki Giovanni, and others.

Randall publishes tapes of poets reading. He publishes a cookbook of African cooking. And he has just started a series of critical books on black poetry. Don Lee, who wrote an excellent introduction to Gwendolyn Brooks's autobiography, has started the critical series with a book of comments on black poetry. Black poets need black critics.

And certainly a premise of Broadside has been that black poets need black publishers, too; something that not all black poets agree with, obviously. But Gwendolyn Brooks has left Harper and Row to come to Broadside. Gwendolyn Brooks, who won the Pulitzer in 1950, did her *Report from Part One* with Broadside last year and thus won the Detroit publisher his first notice in the *New York Times Book Review*.

I think that the best poet Broadside has published is Etheridge Knight. Knight's *Poems from Prison* included the incredible "Ideas of Ancestry," "Hard Rock," and "When You Leave Me." At the end of last year, Broadside brought out his second book, *Belly Song*.

Reading black poetry, a white American surely suffers from the barrier of a common language; and the analogy between the American and English literary traditions holds true, for this common language is not common at all. In the recognition of difference lies the possibility of reading.

THE BLURB WRITER'S FRIEND

In an English magazine called *Poetry Nation*, John Kease has "The Critic's Friend."

It is with considerable pleasure that we present a sentence construction kit from which the critic may develop a wide range of erudite observations on any recently published volume of poetry.

Our 'sentence modules' are based on a Somewhat Improved Modular Prose Linear Extension (SIMPLE) system not previously available to writers in this field.

Sentences may be constructed by linking any four modules from the lists in the sequence 1234. Ambitious critics may find occasional devastating combinations in sequences made from the lists in the order 4321. More rarely, the modules may be ordered 2314 or 2134. These last must be used with great discretion, grammatical errors are possible.

List 1

a) Apathetic extremism on the one hand, together with
b) As a consequence of conflicting Celtic urges
c) Despite emphatic protestations to the contrary
d) Unless the historical base is widened
e) Whilst admitting the validity of current trends
f) None the less it may be postulated that
g) Rich as these particular textures may be
h) Whilst conceding ingenious inflexions
i) This rhetorical question, emphasized by
j) Though 'art may be selective' the passive nature of

List 2

a) critical orthodoxy
b) unselective writing of the polemical variety
c) left-wing preaching to the converted
d) the recent workshop in Bradford
e) a tendency to recondite assumptions
f) his/her over-eagerness to achieve acceptance
g) the pursuit of even supposed concepts
h) symbolic systems and analogical notation
i) the near-extinct oral tradition
j) new nadirs of imaginative 'intensity'

List 3

a) may pre-resonate the situation in relation to
b) can add little to the provincial awareness of
c) ought to modify the approach to
d) will, undoubtedly, aid the confirmation of
e) should intensify the personal hyperbole regarding
f) could crystallise the Modernistic attitude to
g) might yield spontaneous information on
h) must assert a theoretical pressure for
i) re-establishes an Anglo-Welsh insistence on
j) underlines a recidivous pre-occupation with

List 4
a) the need for a stylistic revival
b) *carpe diem*
c) a verse form of unambiguous charm
d) congruence in all Nordic literature
e) an imagery which is both scrupulous and contemporary
f) the possibility of an Arts Council award
g) an essentially heuristic behaviourism
h) Underground 'juvenility'
i) an egalitarian concern with *avant garde* aspirations
j) the recognition that the world is full of phoneys

A most helpful form, which could be useful in this country. First, we would need to Americanize it. For "Celtic," we should read "Workshop" throughout. For "Bradford" read "Cape Cod." For "Anglo-Welsh" read "New Jersey." For "Nordic" read "Buddhist." For "Arts Council" read "Richard Howard."

But I think in America we should adapt Kease's invention for another purpose. When publishers prepare jacket copy for books of poems, they customarily write the poet's famous elder friends, famous former teachers, or famous chance acquaintances, to ask for a few words of friendly testimonial. We are all familiar with the results, since every jacket of every book is crowded with them. (See *Best Blurbs of 1974*.) How much labor could be saved if there were available an Instant Blurb Manufacturing Kit. We could almost adapt Kease's set, but it is far too *critical*. We must increase the Sychophancy Ratio, and the Nacreous Fatuousness Index. Maybe we must make new lists.

Here are four tentative lists, which can be combined as Kease's were combined. There are only five units in each, since blurb-form is more attenuated than book-review form. (The American blurb is as attenuated and

as conventional as the haiku, which it does not other-
wise resemble.)

List 1
a. In reading the magnificent poems of . . . ,
b. Discovering in . . . a new voice,
c. At the same time as . . . is a master of invention,
d. In addition to the splendid ear of . . . ,
e. In the unique gift of a . . . ,

List 2
a. we observe the momentum
b. intelligent readers can discern an embodiment
c. no one can ignore the renaissance
d. we are presented with a creative world
e. it is idle to doubt the existence

List 3
a. of a vital, lively, empathy
b. of esthetic relevance
c. of fresh insight
d. of the startling, individual image
e. of outrageous lyric texture

List 4
a. which displays the presence of genius.
b. which reassures us that poetry thrives.
c. which distills the essence of his/her art.
d. which astonishes us with technical virtuosity.
e. which evokes fluid responses to an unprecedented
   degree.

This kit omits one necessary item, fortunately easy to
supply. A fifth list will offer a pool of names—all of
them respected, elder, famous, authoritative, admired,
and *clean*. The publisher can choose from this pool of
names the right mix. If anyone fears that suitable people
will refuse to lend their names, he should set these fears

aside. A quick look at half a dozen book jackets will lend assurance; many poets will sign their names to anything.

TO JOIN A CLUB

Times and decades enforce dominant artistic modes, and these dominant modes seduce talented artists into forms alien to them—if their egos are not strong enough. Poets and essayists, late in the nineteenth century, broke themselves writing three-volume novels. In earlier times, satire dominated, or verse tragedy, or pastoral verse. Today prose writers direct themselves into nonfiction when their talents might do better in fiction. (E. L. Doctorow's *Ragtime* is the novelist's *revenge* on nonfiction.) Maybe some poets write short-lined, rhapsodic, fantastic, surrealistic free verse when they would do better writing sonnet sequences to Celia.

Of course the *zeitgeist* does not disallow diversity. But the bandwagon (perhaps more accurate a word than *zeitgeist*) never *encourages* diversity, and there is always a bandwagon: the crowd always pushes in one or two directions. I remember when the crowd pushed iambic, archaism, wit, and reference. Now the crowd laughs at them. (The crowd is always laughing.) Richard Wilbur has not abandoned iambic, and iambic has not abandoned him.

In the thirties in England, there were two contrary poles demanding the attention of visual artists. One was Constructivism, in England especially led by Naum Gabo, related to Mondrian's De Stijl and Malevich's Suprematism and the Bauhaus. It was austere, geometric, pure, intellectual, and spiritual. Barbara Hepworth and Ben Nicholson, I suppose, were the two artists best influenced by Constructivism.

On the other hand there was Surrealism, imported nearly intact from France by David Gascoigne, with Herbert Read organizing the criticism. Few people realize the extent of literary Surrealism in the thirties, in England and in America. Soon Penguin will publish an anthology, edited by Edward Germain, which will surprise everybody in its extent and in its quality. Surrealism was wider-spread among literary people in England than among artists, among whom Constructivism took precedence. But Surrealism had its painters and sculptors too, its shows and its advocates.

With an ego as obdurate as stone, Henry Moore kept on carving, and showed with both camps, and learned from both camps. More obviously Surreal—from the late twenties on, his work had involved distortion of the human figure, at any rate, with results that were *at least* as emotional as they were plastic—he made some works *almost* purely Constructivist, and almost lacking organic shape. He carved increasingly expressive figures, during these years, widening and deepening his emotional range, and certainly learned from Surrealist irrationalism at the same time as he learned from Constructivist formalism. He was never pure—not Surrealist nor Constructivist nor anything.

On the other hand, there was a man who had been his great friend when they attended art school in London. I'll call him John Hampstead. They were close friends, they partied and worked together. Hampstead was an extraordinarily gifted portrait painter. His portrait of an old art teacher is lifelike, sensitive, fine, and warm. The delicacy of his brush work, in flesh and fabric, draws you to its texture, and the face is radiant with its own life. Others of his early portraits hang in public galleries. But not late portraits. In the thirties he decided to become a Constructivist, and he gave up portrait painting. He had to be a modern artist, had to be in the swim. And his Constructivism is insensitive, blockish, literal, and head controlled, while his portraits were inward, free, subtle, and emotional. He threw his life away, to join a club.

So the question—obvious by now—is how many poets of fantasy, the neo-Surrealists of *APR, Seneca, Crazy Horse, kayak, The Lamp in the Spine, Iowa, Field, Ohio*; how many would be better poets if they let themselves write in forms temporarily on the index, like blank verse, or narrative, or argument, or sonnets? The same question would be asked of Black Mountain poets, who in their emphasis on line and form resemble the Constructivists. How many of us throw our lives away to join a club?

THE LITERATURE INDUSTRY

AUDEN DIES said the Sunday headlines, *Observer* and *Sunday Times*, as if they were saying GARBO TALKS.

With Auden dead, whom will they elect the new Auden?

The old Auden had stopped writing poetry decades ago, it seems to me. But when the books marched forth, every two or three years, the dutiful reviewers paid dutiful homage. His poems had become crotchety conservative essays and apothegms, couched in bland syllabics— and yet the reviewers dusted off their old admirations, and polished them to look like new.

So whom *will* they elect or crown or appoint the new Auden?

The Literature Industry needs its Audens. It needs

heroes. Heroes sell books, heroes fill magazines which exist to sell books. When Faulkner died, the Literature Industry elected Saul Bellow to replace him. When that election didn't go too well, they elected John Updike and Philip Roth, to form a troika.

The mild, censorious, liberal, skeptical, sentimental, tough, cynical face of Auden—sitting at a table with Lionel Trilling and Jacques Barzun to be photographed in order to influence people to buy books—this face has to be found again, in order to sell more books.

Watch the *New York Times Book Review*. Watch the *New York Review of Books*. Watch *The New Yorker*. Election of the new Auden—Hayden Carruth? Harold Bloom? Charles Bukowski? Everett Aspinwall?—will be announced shortly.

THE MASS CONTEMPT

The *New York Times Book Review* continues to flaunt its contempt for poetry. We used to find fault with the *Book Review* when Francis Brown was editor; we could wish him back, for now the magazine reviews little poetry, reviews it badly (see Christopher Ricks on Galway Kinnell), and mentions poetry in passing only to sneer about it. A little while ago, the *Book Review* printed two columns mentioning books to be published: one week, six hundred words advertised "Fiction" and "Politics"; the next week, five-hundred-and-ninety words covered "History," "Self-Revelation," "Portraits," "Current and Controversial," "Fiction" again, and "Miscellany," before poetry turned up, in the final ten words:

" . . . Oh yes, a new book of poems by Kenneth Rexroth."

Other commercial magazines continue to withdraw from poetry. The *New York Review of Books*, which attended to literature when it began, grudges poetry scant attention now. The *Saturday Review* has stopped publishing poetry altogether. *The New Yorker* has not reviewed poetry since the death of Louise Bogan. If a news magazine pays attention to poetry, it either flatters a fad or suffers jaundice.

(There seem to be many editors in New York who majored in English many years ago. If they ever look at poetry now—raising their eyes momentarily from their vitello tonnato—they resent the notion that Irving Babbitt has ceased to publish. In a recent issue of the American Express magazine, *Travel and Leisure*, the editor—in a column that usually deals with the price of gold chess sets—declared that the National Book Awards ought to be abolished because the 1974 poetry prize went to Allen Ginsberg: "Mr. Ginsburg's poetic style varies between the incompetent and the nonexistent . . . " The editor later apologized for "the misspelling error," as he called it.)

Anyway, poetry thrives without the cooperation of the *New York Times Book Review* or *Travel and Leisure*.

Maybe poetry thrives *because* it lacks this sort of attention. Maybe poetry thrives on an audience which is local and intense. The old metaphor of "audience"— "What has become of the poet's audience?" *Time* used to lament: presumably it was languishing somewhere, along with the snows of yesteryear—has turned literal in the auditoriums and classrooms of the United States.

Printed poetry thrives in personal magazines, and in the efforts of one-man publishers—not in magazines which need a huge circulation. We almost hand our poems around—the way they did it in the seventeenth century.

Goatfoot, Milktongue, Twinbird

The Psychic Origins of Poetic Form

When we pursue the psychic origins of our satisfaction with poetic form, we come to the end of the trail. It is deep in the woods, and there is a fire; Twinbird sits quietly, absorbed in the play of flame that leaps and falls; Goatfoot dances by the fire, his eyes reflecting the orange coals, as his lean foot taps the stone. Inside the fire there is a mother and child, made one, the universe of the red coal. This is Milktongue.

1. Some Premises

First, in connection with oppositions:

1. Any quality of poetry can be used for a number of purposes, including opposed purposes. Thus, concentration on technique has often been used to trivialize content, by poets afraid of what they will learn about themselves. But concentration on technique can absorb the attention while unacknowledged material enters the language; so technique can facilitate inspiration.

On the other hand, a poet can subscribe to an anti-technical doctrine of inspiration in a way that simply substitutes one technique for another. Surrealism can become as formulaic as a pastoral elegy.

2. When a poet says he is doing *north*, look and see if he is not actually doing *south*. Chances are that his bent is so entirely *south* that he must swear total allegiance to *north* in order to include the globe.

3. Energy arises from conflict. Without conflict, no energy. Yin and yang. Dark and light. Pleasure and pain. No synthesis without thesis and antithesis. Conflict of course need not be binary but may include a number of terms.

4. Every present event that moves us deeply connects in our psyches with something (or things) in the past. The analogy is the two pieces of carbon that make an arc light. When they come close enough, the spark leaps across. The one mourning is all mourning; "After the first death, there is no other." This generalization applies to the composition of poems (writing), and to the recomposition of poems (reading).

5. The way out is the same as the way in. To investigate the process of making a poem is not merely an exercise in curiosity or gossip, but an attempt to understand the nature of literature. In the act of reading, the reader undergoes a process—largely without awareness, as the author was largely without intention—which resembles, like a slightly fainter copy of the original, the process of discovery or recovery that the poet went through in his madness or inspiration.

And then, more general:

6. A poem is one man's inside talking to another man's inside. It may *also* be reasonable man talking to reasonable man, but if it is not inside talking to inside, it is not a poem. This inside speaks through the second

language of poetry, the unintended language. Sometimes, as in surrealism, the second language is the only language. It is the ancient prong of carbon in the arc light. We all share more when we are five years old than when we are twenty-five; more at five minutes than at five years. The second language allows poetry to be universal.

7. *Lyric poetry, typically, has one goal and one message, which is to urge the condition of inwardness, the "inside" from which its own structure derives.*

2. Form: the Sensual Body

There is the old false distinction between *vates* and *poiein*. It is a boring distinction, and I apologize for dragging it out again. I want to use it in its own despite.

The *poiein*, from the Greek verb for making or doing, becomes the poet—the master of craft, the maker of the labyrinth of epic or tragedy or lyric hymn, tale-teller and spell-binder. The *vates* is bound in his own spell. He is the rhapsode Socrates patronizes in *Ion*. In his purest form he utters what he does not understand at all, be he oracle or André Breton. He is the visionary, divinely inspired, who like Blake may take dictation from voices.

But Blake's voices returned to dictate revisions. The more intimately we observe any poet who claims extremes of inspiration or of craftsmanship, the more we realize that his claims are a disguise. There is no *poiein* for the same reason that there is no *vates*. The claims may be serious (they may be the compensatory distortion which allows the poet to write at all) and the claims may affect the looks of the poem—a surrealist poem and a neoclassic Imitation of Horace *look* different—but the distinction becomes trivial when we discover the psychic origins of poetic form.

I speak of the psychic origins of poetic *form*. Psychologists have written convincingly of the origins of the *material* of arts, in wish-fulfillment and in the universality of myth. We need not go over ideas of the poet as daydreamer, or of the collective unconsciousness. Ernst Kris's "regression in the service of the ego" names an event but does not explain how it comes about. But one bit of Freud's essay on the poet as daydreamer has been a clue in this search. At the end of his intelligent, snippy paper, Freud says that he lacks time now to deal with form, but that he suspects that formal pleasure is related to forepleasure. Then he ducks through the curtain and disappears. Suppose we consider the implications of his parting shot. Forepleasure develops out of the sensuality of the whole body which the infant experiences in the pleasure of the crib and of the breast. The connection between forepleasure and infancy is the motion from rationality to metaphor.

But to begin our search for the psychic origins of poetic form, we must first think of what is usually meant by the word "form," and then we must look for the reality. So often form is looked upon only as the fulfillment of metrical expectations. Meter is nothing but a loose set of probabilities; it is a trick easily learned; anyone can learn to arrange one-hundred-and-forty syllables so that the even syllables are louder than the odd ones, and every tenth syllable rhymes: the object will be a sonnet. But only when you have forgotten the requirements of meter do you begin to write poetry in it. The resolutions of form which ultimately provide the wholeness of a poem—resolutions of syntax, metaphor, diction, and sound—are minute and subtle and vary from poem to poem. They vary from sonnet to sonnet, or, equally and not more greatly, from sonnet to free verse lyric.

Meter is no more seriously binding than the frame we put around a picture. But the *form* of free verse is as binding and as liberating as the *form* of a rondeau. Free verse is simply less predictable. Yeats said that the finished poem made a sound like the click of the lid on a perfectly made box. One-hundred-and-forty syllables, organized into a sonnet, do not necessarily make a click; the same number of syllables, dispersed in asymmetric lines of free verse, will click like a lid if the poem is good. In the sonnet and in the free verse poem, the poet improvises toward that click, and achieves his resolution in unpredictable ways. The rhymes and line-lengths of the sonnet are too gross to contribute greatly to that sense of resolution. The click is our sense of lyric *form*. This pleasure in resolution is Twinbird.

The wholeness and identity of the completed poem, the poem as object in time, the sensual body of the poem—this wholeness depends upon a complex of unpredictable fulfillments. The satisfying resolutions in a sonnet are more subtle than rhyme and meter, and less predictable. The body of sound grows in resolutions like assonance and alliteration, and in near-misses of both; or in the alternations, the going-away and coming-back, of fast and slow, long and short, high and low. The poet—free verse or meter, whatever—may start with lines full of long vowels, glide on diphthong sounds like "eye" and "ay" for instance, move to quick alternative lines of short vowels and clipped consonants, and return in a coda to the long vowels "eye" and "ay." The assonance is shaped like a saucer.

The requirements of fixity are complex, and the conscious mind seldom deals with them. Any poet who has written metrically can write arithmetically correct iambic pentameter as fast as his hand can move. In improvising towards the click, the poet is mostly aware of what sounds right and what does not. When something persists in not sounding right, the poet can examine it bit by bit—can analyze it—in the attempt to consult his knowledge and apply it.

This knowledge is habitual. It is usually not visible to the poet, but it is available for consultation. When you learn something so well that you forget it, you can begin to do it. You dance best when you forget that you are dancing. Athletics—a tennis stroke, swimming, a receiver catching a football—is full of examples of actions done as if by instinct, which are actually learned procedure, studied and practiced until they become "second nature." So it is with poetry. The literary form of poems is created largely by learning—in collaboration with the unconscious by a process I will talk about later. Possible resolutions of metaphor, diction, and sound are coded into memory from our reading of other poets, occasionally from our reading of criticism, from our talk with other poets, and from our revisions of our own work, with the conscious analysis that this revision sometimes entails. New resolutions are combinations of parts of old ones, making new what may later be combined again and made new again.

When the experienced reader takes a poem in, his sense of fixity comes also from memory. He too has the codes in his head. The new poem fulfills the old habits of expectation in some unexpected way. The reader does not know why—unless he bothers to analyze; then probably not fully—he is pleased by the sensual body of the poem. He does not need to know why, unless he must write about it. The pleasure is sufficient. Since the poet's madness is the reader's madness, the resolution of the mad material is the reader's resolution as well as the poet's. The way in is the same as the way out.

Whatever else we may say of a poem we admire, it exists as a sensual body. It is beautiful and pleasant, manifest content aside, like a worn stone that is good to touch, or like a shape of flowers arranged or accidental. This sensual body reaches us through our mouths, which are warm in the love of vowels held together, and in the muscles of our legs which as in dance tap the motion and pause of linear and syntactic structure. These pleasures are Milktongue and Goatfoot.

There is a nonintellectual beauty in the moving together of words in phrases—"the music of diction"—and in resolution of image and metaphor. The sophisticated reader of poetry responds quickly to the sensual body of a poem, before he interrogates the poem at all. The pleasure we feel, reading a poem, is our assurance of its integrity. (So Pound said that technique is the test of sincerity.) We will glance through a poem rapidly and if it is a skillful fake we will feel repelled. If the poem is alive and honest, we will feel assent in our quickening pulse—though it might take us some time to explain what we were reacting to.

The soi-disant *vates* feels that he speaks from the unconscious (or with the voice of the God), and the *poiein* that he makes all these wholenesses of shape on purpose. Both of them disguise the truth. All poets are *poiein* and *vates*. The *poiein* comes from memory of reading, and the *vates* from memory of infancy. The sensual body of the poem derives from memory of reading most obviously, but ultimately it leads us back further—to the most primitive psychic origins of poetic form.

3. Conflict Makes Energy

People frequently notice that poetry concerns itself with unpleasant subjects: death, deprivation, loneliness, despair, if love then the death of love, and abandonment. Of course there are happy poems, but in English poetry there are few which are happy through and through—and those few tend to be light, short, pleasant, and forgettable. Most memorable happy poems have a portion of blackness in them. Over all—Keats, Blake, Donne, Yeats, Eliot, Shakespeare, Wordsworth—there is more dark than light, more elegy than celebration. There is no great poem in our language which is simply happy.

Noticing these facts, we reach for explanations: maybe to be happy is to be a simpleton; maybe poets are morbid; maybe life is darker than it is light; maybe when you are happy you are too busy being happy to write poems about it and when you are sad, you write poems in order to *do* something. There may be half-truths in these common ideas, but the real explanation lies in the structure of a poem; and, I suggest, in the structure of human reality.

Energy arises from conflict.

A) The sensual body of a poem is a pleasure separate from any message the poem may contain.

B) If the poem contains a message which is pleasurable (a word I have just substituted for "happy"), then the two pleasures walk agreeably together for a few feet, and collapse into a smiling lethargy. The happy poem sleeps in the sun.

C) If the message of the poem, on the whole, is terrifying—that They flee from me, that one time did me seek; that I am sick, I must die; that On Margate Sands/I can connect/Nothing with nothing; that Things fall apart, the center will not hold—then pain of message and pleasure of body copulate in a glorious conflict-dance of energy. This alternation of pleasure and pain is so swift as to seem simultaneous, to *be* simultaneous in the complexity both of creation and reception, a fused circle of yin and yang, a oneness in diversity.

The pain is clear to anyone. The pleasure is clear (dear) to anyone who loves poems. If we acknowledge the pleasure of the sensual body of the poem, we can see why painful poems are best: conflict makes energy and resolves our suffering into ambivalent living tissue. If human nature is necessarily ambivalent, then the structure of the energetic poem resembles the structure of human nature.

The sensual body, in poems, is not simply a compensation for the pain of the message. It is considerably more important, and more central to the nature of poetry. When we pursue the psychic origins of our satisfaction with poetic form, we come to the end of the trail. It is deep in the woods, and there is a fire; Twinbird sits quietly, absorbed in the play of flame that leaps and falls; Goatfoot dances by the fire, his eyes reflecting the orange coals, as his lean foot taps the stone. Inside the fire there is a mother and child, made one, the universe of the red coal. This is Milktongue.

4. Goatfoot, Milktongue, Twinbird

Once at a conference on creativity, a young linguist presented a model of language. Xeroxed in outline, it was beautiful like a concrete poem. I looked for language as used in poems and looked a long time. Finally I found it, under "autistic utterance," with the note that this utterance might later be refined into lyric poetry. It reminded me of another conference I had attended a year or two earlier. A psychoanalyst delivered a paper on deriving biographical information about an author from his fiction. He distributed mimeographed copies of his paper, which his secretary had typed from his obscure handwriting; he began his remarks by presenting a list of errata. The first correction was, "For 'autistic,' read 'artistic' throughout."

The newborn infant cries, he sucks at the air until he finds the nipple. At first he finds his hand to suck by accident—fingers, thumb; then he learns to repeat that pleasure. Another mouth-pleasure is the autistic babble, the "goo-goo," the small cooing and purring and bubbling. These are sounds of pleasure; they are without message, except that a parent interprets them as "happy": pleasure is happy. Wittgenstein once said that we could sing the song with expression or without expression; very well, he said, let us have the expression without the song. (He was being ironic; I am not.) The baby's autistic murmur is the expression without the song. His small tongue curls around the sounds, the way his tongue warms with the tiny thread of milk that he pulls from his mother. This is Milktongue, and in poetry it is the deep and primitive pleasure of vowels in the mouth, of assonance and of holds on adjacent long vowels; of consonance, mmmm, and alliteration. It is Dylan Thomas and the curlew cry; it is That dolphintorn, that gong-tormented sea; it is Then, in a wailful choir, the small gnats mourn.

As Milktongue mouths the noises it curls around, the rest of his body plays in pleasure also. His fists open and close spasmodically. His small bowed legs, no good for walking, contract and expand in a rhythmic beat. He has begun the dance, his muscles move like his heartbeat, and Goatfoot improvises his circle around the fire. His whole body throbs and thrills with pleasure. The first parts of his body which he notices are his hands; then his feet. The strange birds fly at his head, waver, and pause. After a while he perceives that there are two of them. They begin to act when he wishes them to act, and since the *mental* creates the *physical*, Twinbird is the first magic he performs. He examines these independent/dependent twin birds. They are exactly alike. And they are exactly unalike, mirror images of each other, the perfection of opposite-same.

As the infant grows, the noises split off partly into messages. "Mmm" can be milk and mother. "Da-da" belongs to another huge shape. He crawls and his muscles become useful to move him toward the toy and the soda cracker. Twinbird flies more and more at his will, as Milktongue speaks, and Goatfoot crawls. But still he rolls on his back and his legs beat in the air. Still, the sister hands flutter at his face. Still, the noises without message fill the happy time of waking before hunger, and the softening down, milktongue full, into sleep. The growing child skips rope, hops, dances to a music outside intelligence, rhymes to the hopscotch or jump rope, and listens to the sounds his parents please him with:

> Pease porridge hot
> Pease porridge cold
> Pease porridge in-the-pot
> Five days old.

Or himself learns:

> Bah, bah, black sheep
> Have you any wool;
> Yes, sir, yes, sir,
> Three bags full.
> One for my master,
> One for my dame
> And one for the little boy
> That lives down the lane.

The mouth-pleasure, the muscle-pleasure, the pleasure of match-unmatch.

But "Shades of the prison house begin to close/Upon the growing boy." Civilized humans try gradually to cut away the autistic component in their speech. Goatfoot survives in the dance, Twinbird in rhyme and resolution of dance and noise. Milktongue hides itself more. It ties us to the mother so obviously that men are ashamed of it. Tribal society was unashamed and worshipped Milktongue in religion and history. Among the outcast in the modern world, Milktongue sometimes endures in language, as it does in the American black world, and in the world of the poor Southern whites. In Ireland where the mother (and the Virgin) are still central, Milktongue remains in swearing and in the love of sweet speech. Probably, in most of the modern world, Milktongue exists only in smoking, eating, and drinking; and in oral sexuality.

But Milktongue and Goatfoot and Twinbird have always lived in the lyric poem, for poet and for reader. They are the ancestors, and they remain the psychic origins of poetic form, primitive both personally (back to the crib) and historically (back to the fire in front of the cave). They keep pure the sensual pleasure that is the dark secret shape of the poem. We need an intermediary to deal with them, for a clear reason: Goatfoot and Milktongue and Twinbird, like other figures that inhabit the forest, are wholly preverbal. They live before words.

They approach the edge of the clearing, able to come close because the Priestess has no eyes to frighten them with. The Priestess, built of the memory of old pleasures, only knows how to select and order. The Priestess does not know what she says, but she knows that she says it in dactylic hexameter. Goatfoot and Milktongue and Twinbird leave gifts at the edge of the forest. The

Priestess picks up the gifts, and turns to the light, and speaks words that carry the dark mysterious memory of the forest and the pleasure.

The poet writing, and the reader reading, lulled by Goatfoot and Milktongue and Twinbird into the oldest world, become able to think as the infant thinks, with transformation and omnipotence and magic. The form of the poem, because it exists separately from messages, can act as trigger or catalyst or enzyme to activate not messages but types of mental behavior. Coleridge spoke of meter as effecting the willing suspension of disbelief. They are the three memories of the body—not only meter; and they are powerful magic—not only suspension of disbelief. The form of the poem unlocks the mind to old pleasures. Pleasure leaves the mind vulnerable to the content of experience before we have intellectualized the experience and made it acceptable to the civilized consciousness. The form allows the mind to encounter real experience, and so the real message is permitted to speak—but only because the figures in the forest, untouched by messages, have danced and crooned and shaped.

The release of power and sweetness! Milktongue also remembers hunger, and the cry without answer. Goatfoot remembers falling, and the ache that bent the night. Twinbird remembers the loss of the brother, so long he believed in abandonment forever. From the earliest times, poetry has existed in order to retrieve, to find again, and to release. In the man who writes the poem, in the reader who lives it again, in the ideas, the wit, the images, the doctrines, the exhortations, the laments and the cries of joy, the lost forest struggles to be born again inside the words. The life or urge and instinct, that rages and coos, kicks and frolics, as it chooses only without choosing—this life is the life the poem grows from, and leans toward.

The Line

The Line most obviously bodies forth the dance—the pause, balance, and sudden motion—that is Goatfoot. At line-end—by altering pitch or lengthening the hold of a vowel or of a consonant—the Line is Milktongue. By giving us units which we hold against each other, different and the same—and by isolating the syllable which rhymes, different and the same—the Line is Twinbird.

By invoking Goatfoot, Milktongue, and Twinbird, the Line is wholly serious, because it allows us to use parts of the mind usually asleep. When we take a lined poem and put it into paragraphs, we remove imagination and energy, we create banality. John Haines used this example; I use it again. It is no insult to William Carlos Williams, or to his poem, to say that the prose sentence, "So much depends upon a red wheelbarrow, glazed with rain water, beside the white chickens," is boring. The Line brings forth the etymological wit (depends/upon; wheel/barrow). The Line brings forth the assonance only half-heard in the prose: "Glazed/rain"; "beside/ white"). And in fact the Line (in this poem and not in every poem) is an *intellectual* force, insisting on particularity by the value it gives to isolated words of sense.

When a critic takes a lined poem and prints it as prose,

A series of articles in *Field* discussed the poetic line.

in order to show that the poem is inferior, he tells us nothing about the poem. (This series of notes began in response to a reviewer, in the *Hudson Review*, who tried to denigrate poems by Charles Simic and John Haines by printing them as prose.) Such a critic reveals that he is ignorant or disingenuous. Back in the silly wars about free verse, toward the end of the First World War, American critics who wished to prove that free verse was only prose took poems by Ezra Pound (or Amy Lowell) and printed them as prose. "See," they said triumphantly, like the man in the *Hudson Review*, "it's only prose." They only proved that they had no sense of the Line.

A sense of the Line disappeared from common knowledge some time ago. In 1765, an Englishman named John Rice proposed breaking Milton's lines according to sense, and not according to the pentameter, presumably changing:

> Of man's first disobedience, and the fruit
> Of that forbidden tree, whose mortal taste
> Brought death into the world, and all our woe,
> With loss of Eden, till one greater man
> Restore us, and regain the blissful seat,
> Sing heavenly muse . . .

to:

> Of man's first disobedience
> And the fruit
> Of that forbidden tree
> Whose mortal taste
> Brought death into the world
> And all our woe
> With loss of Eden
> Till one greater man
> Restore us
> And regain the blissful seat,
> Sing heavenly muse . . .

This rewriting of Milton resembles bad free verse, which is usually bad rhythmically *because* the poet has no sense of the line as a melodic unit. The lines are short and coincidentally semantic and phonic. But Milton— need I say—is not damaged by this crude rearrangement. Damage only occurs to the critic (John Rice) who thinks that line structure does not matter, or to the reviewer who thinks that the poem must prove itself apart from its lineation—which is to think that line structure does not matter.

A hundred years earlier, John Rice's ear would have been more reliable. With the increase of literacy, and the vast increase in printed books of prose, people began to read poetry without pausing at the ends of lines. The Line I suppose was originally mnemonic. As far as I can tell, actors indicated line-structure by pause and pitch at least through Shakespeare's time, probably until the closing of the theatres. Complaints from old fashioned play-goers—that upstart actors like David Garrick no longer paused where the poet indicated that they should pause—occur in the eighteenth century. It is possible to connect literacy, capitalism, and puritanism with this insult to Goatfoot.

Of course the Line has continued to exist, even among certain actors, and among all good poets. *You cannot read Keats or Hardy or Pound as if they were prose without losing a connection to the unconscious mind, a connection made by sound.* Maybe the reason people *want* to speak poetry as prose, and therefore to belittle the Line, is that they are frightened of the psychic interior to which the Line, inhabiting mouth and muscle, may lead them. Such a reason would explain the way many professors of English read poetry aloud.

To speak with such seriousness of the Line is not to

deny the frequency in poetry of other, perhaps vaguer things: metaphor, image, thought, and whatever people mean by "tension" or "density." But Williams writes without metaphor on occasion, Creeley writes sometimes without images, and Mother Goose writes poems with little thought. Mother Goose, who is all mouth and muscle, is a better poet than W. H. Auden.

Words without Bodies

Gregory Orr, as it happens, is one of the healthier events in recent American poetry. Among the very young poets (say, younger than Charles Simic), he seems to me the best explorer of dream images or fantasy. (Ai is a wonderful poet of waking life.) Too many poets, now, seem to use a light-headed, goofy sort of fantasy as a gymnasium to do tricks in. Gregory Orr, on the other hand, starts from *dream as necessity*, as life-giving rather than life-enhancing. The dream is his way to come alive. There is an urgency to his fantasy. The urgency comes from the fact that his fantasy is therapeutic and not decorative.

However, I want to take a remark of his as a danger sign for poetry.

Orr remarks that the people he has been reading lately do not write in English. "The poets I've been affected by most powerfully recently are all foreign: Zbigniew Herbert, Yehudi Amichai, Transtrommer, Georg Trakl. Perhaps that says something: that my interest is more in the presentation of states of consciousness than it is in language itself. The language is important, but to me there is something more important under it/beyond it that I want to get to . . ."

It's true, there is the poetry of images, which translates well. Neruda, Trakl, Amichai, Transtrommer, Herbert. On the other hand, there is also the poetry of wit, syntax, and metrics which translates poorly: Valery, Pushkin, Goethe.

I will not argue the relative value of contrasting sorts of poetry. I suspect that the argument would lead nowhere.

Orr's sentences remind us that two common saws about poetry are simply not true: in my generation, we told each other endlessly how Mallarmé told Dégas that poetry was not written with ideas, but with words: and we quoted Robert Frost defining poetry as whatever got lost in translation.

Okay. Poetry is not just written in words. And poetry does not entirely get lost in translation. Or at least, not all poetry gets lost in translation.

But something does get lost in translation, even from Neruda, even from Trakl, even from Herbert, Amichai, Transtrommer. People who read the originals show me, convince me, indicate to me by repetition and by pronunciation and by exhortation, that the originals have qualities that the translations lack. For that matter, I can find out for myself; too many people have forgotten Pound's lesson, that you can learn more by trying to read the original with a dictionary and a grammar book and a linguistic friend than you can from the best literary translation.

But when you read much of the poetry by young Americans, and some young Englishmen also, you realize that their writing is based upon their reading of translations. That is, much of contemporary American poetry is not written in words. It is written as if *for* translation. It is plain, it is flat, and it is nothing but images. It is a grave danger to young poets that they may become so obsessed by the centrality of the deep or universal or archetypal image that they will abandon—or ignore, or deny the existence of—the dark mouth of the vowel by which the image tells its sensual rune.

Notes on Robert Bly and
Sleepers Joining Hands

This is not a "review," partly because transitions are fatuous; transitions and order translate "notes" into "review" or "article." And partly because I have no objectivity. This poet has been my friend for twenty-five years.

Bly is the most systematic poet in the United States. Gary Snyder is second. Both men are learned, eclectic priests. Both are born teachers, neither teaches at a college. Snyder is more accurate than Bly, in his learning; Bly is wilder in his weddings of the unweddable. Bly is more inclusive; Snyder only recently approaches the west, by way of cave paintings; Bly moves like a huge hummingbird from Jung flower to Zen flower, from the Buddha to the Great Mother. Snyder writes lines loving the motion and the feel of language. Bly seems mostly unaware of this pleasure. If Bly could write his poems in amino acids or bird calls, he would just as lief; the spirit matters to him, and not the shoulders of consonants.

Twenty years ago, before he had published poems to anyone's notice, Bly started to write a series of books of poems with titles like *The Road to Poverty and Death*.

These books represented different stages of the soul's journey. At first, the books were rather thin. They have become fuller, over the years. Bly has increased his range, his openness; the style of his poems has loosened; he has written prose poems; he has learned a lot from his reading; he is able to write at length now—but is still writing the books he began to write decades ago.

The other poet of the soul's journey, since Roethke's death, is Galway Kinnell. And he is perhaps the most unsystematic of poets.

One of the books that began to emerge was something that Bly referred to as "the country poems," in conversation. When a considerable group of country poems had been written, they appeared as a book called *Silence in the Snowy Fields*. The *Silence* poems are soft and frequently happy, even in their melancholy somehow secure. They are the less complicated, more primitive aspect of Bly's vision, and therefore appropriately the first to be published. They are psychically the earliest, approaching the uruboros.

When *The Light around the Body* came out, people were offended. We don't want our poets to change.

But Bly hadn't changed at all.

If the readers had noticed the old J. P. Morgan poems in *New World Writing*, they would have seen the politics of the outer world judged by the standards of the inner world—and years before Vietnam. And if they had looked into magazines and anthologies, where Bly for years had published poems which he did not choose to include in *Silence*, they would have seen poems about the phallic violence of the patriarchs, and they would have seen the dislocations of surrealism.

Many of the frightening poems of *Light around the Body* were older than many of the gentle poems of

Silence. The Vietnam war did not change Bly's ideas. The Vietnam war was the horrifying embodiment of the "father of rocks," the "father of cheerfulness," which he had named years before.

A lot of bad political poetry has been written, poetry which proclaims the virtue of the poet in his convictions about wars in Asia.

Do you all agree? Please don't agree quite so quickly! Bad as these political poems have been, the criticism of political poetry has been worse. Literary and academic people are *terrified* whenever an artist expresses an opinion.

Bly's poems do not attest to Bly's virtue. (Some of Bly's political actions outside the writing of poems seem to me virtuous indeed, both courageous and useful. Naturally he has been ridiculed and sneered at by hacks and cowards, but that is no matter.) The point about Bly's political poems is clear or ought to be: the violence is Bly's own. Certainly he understands his own murderousness, and no man can protest war if he does not understand himself a murderer.

Bly's moral judgments about the war in Asia derive from his general system, visible even in *Silence*, and his moral judgment is not *ad hoc*. *Ad hoc* judgments evaporate under pressure. Bly's judgments would survive the flames and the stake.

Sleepers is the best of the three books, and is synthetic. It recapitulates the first two books and takes a further step. The further step *depends* on the ideas in the prose, and *occurs* in the long title poem that ends the book. Still, the ideas of the prose, like the accidents of history in the political poems, find room only in a mind that is already prepared for them. Bly had written "A Man

Writes to a Part of Himself" a decade before he read Neumann. And though Neumann's ideas helped the long poem to evolve, parts of it are as old as anything he has ever printed. The poem was begun when he was in his twenties.

The first section includes more country poems—the privacy poems, the shack poems—with their wonderful moments of intuitive connection:

> When I woke, new snow had fallen.
> I am alone, yet someone else is with me,
> Drinking coffee, looking out at the snow.

This intuition is basic to the despair elsewhere. Without the memory or knowledge of connection, how do we feel separation? "And how did this separation come about?"

"Water under the Earth" and "Hair" began as portions of the long title poem, but after considerable struggle were removed to stand alone. Since the whole of Bly's work is one poem, the decision is less crucial than it would be for most poets.

Bly's connectedness with all things, his systematic and evolutionary empathy, never shows better than in some lines from "Water under the Earth."

> I am only half-risen.
> I see how carefully I have covered my tracks as
> I wrote,
> How well I brushed over the past with my tail.
> I enter rooms full of photographs of the dead.
> My hair stands up
> As a badger crosses my path in the moonlight.

And this first section ends with the Teeth Mother poem, mistakenly considered a poem "about" Vietnam and therefore unread in the very act of being read. It is a poem of vast and general intelligence, a poem created out of the knowledge of *history* surely, but psychic history and geopolitical history made one as they must be made.

The prose passages, "I Came Out of the Mother Naked," are crucial to any understanding of Bly's ideas. Bly takes them as literal and historical: nobody should forget this reality. Myself, I remember the voices conversing with Yeats. "Shall I give up poetry and promulgate your doctrines?" "No! No! We come to give you metaphors for poetry!"

If it be understood, for heaven's sake, those "metaphors for poetry" have the reality of flesh, and the imprint of spirit.

Relative to metaphor, history is mere decoration.

"Sleepers Joining Hands" is the earliest and latest of Bly's work. It has taken this long for him to use material which leaves him so vulnerable:

> . . . I sent my brother away.
> I saw him turn and leave. It was a schoolyard.
> I gave him to the dark people passing.
> He learned to sleep alone on the high buttes.
> I heard he was near the Missouri, taken in by the
> traveling Sioux . . .

In this poem, Bly talks of the presence of the fathers in him who drive the shadow away, fathers of spiritual pride and arrogance. And he speaks of his own suffering, and the suffering of others:

I see the birds inside me,
with massive shoulders, like humpbacked Puritan ministers,
a headstrong beak ahead,
and wings supple as the stingray's,
ending in claws, lifting over the shadowy peaks.

Looking down, I see dark marks on my shirt.
My mother gave me that shirt, and hoped that her son
     would be the one man in the world
who would have a happy marriage,
but look at me now—
I have been divorced five hundred times,
six hundred times yesterday alone.

I hear the sound of hoofs . . . coming . . . Now the men
move in, smashing and burning. The huts
of the Shadowy People are turned over, the wood
utensils broken, straw mats set on fire,
digging sticks jumped on, clay bowls
smashed with dropped stones . . . .

It is a great journey poem, the journey through the
horrors of loneliness in New York City, through the
joys of solitude, and the spiritual selfishness possible to
solitude, and into the present life:

What I have written is not good enough.
Who does it help?
I am ashamed sitting on the edge of my bed.

I think that Bly has more to write, within the scope of
this poem—though it does not matter exactly whether
it occurs in expanding this poem or in further work.
This poem is very beautiful, and the best of Bly's work.
But parts of the journey are still unwritten, parts of the
journey that move from the original loss and despair,
and the later spiritual withdrawal, into the condition of
the end of the poem:

All the sleepers in the world join hands.

We do not have the whole journey. We have a synopsis, almost. It will take the rest of a lifetime to make the metaphors that are the footsteps of this journey, which is the journey to a good death.

An Interview

With Stanley Plumly and Wayne Dodd

If you were to update the introduction to your Penguin anthology of contemporary American poetry, which is about ten or eleven years old, what would you say now about what is happening in contemporary American poetry? What prophecies have been fulfilled, if any?

I couldn't update the introduction. I would have to start over again. That essay organized some thoughts in 1961 or 1962; my thoughts are different now; they always would be, in any five year period. In connection with that introduction, I used to think of something Jarrell said about a prediction of his own: that he felt like the weatherman who predicted rain, and then there was a flood which wiped out an entire county. . . . In 1961, I said that the poetry of fantasy was the new thing in American poetry. By 1971, it seemed almost an embarrassment. For a while, I came to think that any-body *good*, who was in his twenties, would have to write poetry which was totally *un*fantastic—a poetry of description, facts, or history maybe. Then Gregory Orr comes along, and I am wholly wrong. Gratefully. In fact, there are a number of good people continuing the tradition—as well as all the little imitators. Russell Edson is very good. Charles Simic. Hell, this was not some *fashion* that I was talking about. This is the main tradition of poetry for the last hundred years. More than that, fantasy—expressionism, surrealism, symbolism often—is one of the major modes of poetry always. Look. Poetry has been with us about four thousand years. What is it up to, in all that time? It does not try to go back to the uruboros—whatever the poets tell you they're doing—but it does try to synthesize prelapsarian and postlapsarian states of man. Poetry is evolutionary.

How do you argue that?

Poetry does what has to be done. The last step in evolution was to move from instinctual behavior—Yeats's golden unity, no separation between thought and action—to lighting fires to scare elephants into swamps, to the development of the cerebral cortex, to everything that gets labeled "reason" or "logic" by people who are not philosophers. That was the last great step, which allowed civilization to happen. And that was the Fall of man. Erich Fromm says that the Fall was a move from rural to urban Babylon some three thousand years ago. I think the Fall was more like forty thousand years ago. Maybe longer. Anyway, the next great step must recover the order of intensity, must *add* it to the order of chronology. *Add* the order of immediacy to the order of sizes, *add* intuitive order to rational order. The poem embodies the synthesis. The poem is not a two-part thing, it's a single thing. It embodies the synthesis because it uses *language*, and the unconscious does *not talk*: sometimes we speak of surrealist poetry as if it were the unconscious actually speaking. Language and syntax are cerebral, coming from the cerebral cortex. Language is not something bears and alligators use. Once something speaks, that thing is not the unconscious.

How would you define this last hundred years, this European tradition which you say now has become American property . . . ?

Oh, it's not just American property. It's international.

Yes, it's international. But we were closed to it so long.

I don't know that we were. I used to think that there was total discontinuity between Eliot and Pound and what happens now. I no longer think so. Perhaps I needed to think that way. If your father existed, you would have to kill him, so it was easier to insist that your father didn't exist. Now maybe we can read *The Waste Land* as a surrealist poem—at least with a small s. Certainly it's not some historical, Christian assemblage of ironies. And Pound, in the later *Cantos*, in the images of light—the great acorn of light—makes an intuition of synthesis.

When you speak of the last hundred years, are you talking about French Symbolists, or theoreticians?

Not only that. I am saying poetry makes this intuitional synthesis *by its nature*. Poetry takes language, which is cerebral, and builds the body into it, the muscles and the mouth: the muscles like the leg dancing, the mouth like sucking at a teat.

Is there room in your theory of the nature of poetry for poetry to be different? *For the last four thousand years, surely there have been stages in the development of consciousness. Would poetry be different, according to the stage of the development of consciousness?*

In the overview, I don't think that poetry has varied

enormously in the last four thousand years. Of course style has changed. Style has changed not by reflecting the development of consciousness, but by reflecting the development of social systems. Poetry is Mother Goose and poetry is John Donne. Both make the synthesis I describe. Both do other things, separate things. But if Mother Goose and John Donne do the same thing in relationship to consciousness, then I would say that consciousness is not changing rapidly enough for me to notice it.

How about between Homer and John Donne?

If you get down with your nose to the ground and look at the contour of the land, the contour varies like mountains and canyons. If you sit on a jet six miles up in the air, the land looks flatter. From the distance of the sun, the earth is smoother than a bowling ball.

Would you never at one moment say, "I think this is what poetry is, and what it is doing and where it is going"?

Well, you can try to predict *style*, if predicting style turns you on. I guess sometimes it has turned me on, come to think of it. It's fun, but it's not serious.

Do you think that in the past decade and a half, there has occurred among American poets a basic alteration of spiritual or emotional or psychical consciousness? I mean an opening up to the possibilities that poetry has always had?

Yes. In the last two decades, there has been great change. And the change has been precisely to move into the main stream, the stream which the *genre* of lyric poetry has always affirmed. Twenty years ago, it seems to me, everybody I knew, certainly including me—maybe especially me—was extremely parochial, extremely *local* in the idea of writing a poem. Witwork. In the overview, that time seems a small aberration in the history of American poetry, in the hundred and twenty years since the "Song of Myself." Nowadays, poets seem to be much more properly ambitious. There are silly things going on in American poetry right now, but silly things tend to disappear, so in the long run they don't matter. I mean an epidemic of know-nothingism, somehow or other proliferated by MFA programs. We have the creative-writing industry. People of minimal talents manage an MFA, and then go out and teach people of less talent, who continue to scrape through, and standards get lower and lower. Then because there is so much writing going on, and because there are jobs for writers at universities, and so much need to publish, they start editing magazines and publishing each other. There's an emphasis on *quantity* production, quantity publication. I'm astonished sometimes at how a poet with talent, who seems sophisticated, will take *quantity* seriously. Recently I had a flyer from a young poet, something he sends out when he wants to do poetry readings, in which he had printed that he had published, say, something like four hundred and twenty-seven poems in the last three years.

What would you say, as an old friend of Robert Bly, has been Bly's effect on the direction of American poetry?

I'm not sure I say this as an old friend of Robert Bly. But I say it *and* I'm an old friend of Robert Bly. His effect has been huge, and it has been healthy. He has had his effect as a conduit, as a source of information and of extended range—most obviously in his translations from 30,000 different languages. He is fundamentally *generous*. He brings to American poetry so much that most Americans overlook. And also he brings to the discussion of poetry all sorts of other disciplines, from brain research to anthropology. I don't care if he gets his facts wrong. He has, as he has been known to admit, a deficient sense of fact. He mistakes his sources, gets his facts wrong—and says exactly the right thing. Oh, the energy of his analogies! The intellectual *energy*! He's like a thousand horses stampeding.

Are other contemporary poets important to you?

Yes, they are. We are important to each other. For me, the most important poets of my own age are Robert Bly, preeminently; and Louis Simpson and Galway Kinnell and W. D. Snodgrass and James Wright; and many others I see less often, like Gary Snyder, Robert Creeley, Adrienne Rich; and younger ones, too. I hope that we can become more important to each other still, as we grow older. One of the troubles with American poets, as they age, is that they become lost in the spaces of this country, they become lonely, they die alone in hotel rooms. I'm determined that we not go through what our elders have gone through. The generation of people born around the time of the first world war has destroyed itself.

Some things that people say can stay with you forever. Once I was talking with Galway Kinnell. I was praising certain young poets who are funny and light and irreverent and so on. Galway got to look darker and darker, and did not speak, as he has a way of doing. *Not*

doing. Finally he said, very slowly, "I don't have ...
any interest ... in any poem ... to which the poet ...
didn't bring the whole ... of his life to bear ... at the
moment of writing." That's a big order. When Galway
said it, I recognized that it was really how I wanted to
be. I hope to live up to it. When Galway said it, he was
in the middle of working on *The Book of Nightmares*.
He did it. It's a moral idea of the poem, the moral neces-
sity to struggle to the end of things. If you begin with
something that has echoes of the old connections, you
are faced with various choices, in the long process of
writing the poem. You don't always know you are
making these choices. You have to learn to know. In a
way, we must become *more* conscious in the long pro-
cess of writing the poem. You must cut out something
which does not belong. More importantly, and with
more difficulty, when you find a wall ... well, you have
to tear down the wall, and *break* in there, and find out
what is there. What you find inside, what you find when
you break down the wall, may be quite horrible—rows
and rows of skeletons chained to the wall.

That's a conscious act?

It's a conscious act of opening yourself to go back to
the origins of your word. You cannot create what you
find when you break down the wall. But you can create
the breaking.

*My perception of your work is that you have steadily
moved in this direction.*

Not steadily. I hope at least sporadically. As I look back
there seem so many detours, all sorts of evasions, so

much wasted time. I am not happy with what I've done in the last five or six years. I dislike *The Yellow Room*.

Why?

It's evasive. It isn't hard enough. There's too much left out.

You don't think it makes you vulnerable enough?

People who reviewed it kept saying that I was vulnerable. But it was not in fact *open* enough. I dislike it for what I did not say, more than for what I did say. Also, something else happened in the writing of that book— something which seems separate from the question of vulnerability or openness. You should never pay attention to reviews, to the opinions generally held about you. But you do. One thing that has been said about me from the beginning has been that I was merely a technician. *A Roof of Tiger Lilies* was reviewed as if I were some sort of freak of nature, a frozen monster of technique. Perfection, and no feelings. (Actually, if you checked out the reviews, you wouldn't probably find anything like this at all. Everybody has a weird idea of his own reviews. Nobody ever gets praise enough!) Well, I've always cared immensely about the movement of the line. About the sounds I make. Still do, and I think it's *all right*. But for a while maybe I listened to the reviewers too closely. And when I was working on *The Yellow Room*, of course I was in the middle of the love affair that that poem is about. That woman always praised feelings as opposed to ideas, as if they were in some sort of battle—which they were in her, I suppose.

I do like a few of the poems in that book. I like the

one at the end. But many of the others seem to me to refuse to break down that wall. And they also refuse to be careful in a way which is in fact a violation of my relationship with the Muse. Because that kind of "carefulness" is a sensual love of the motion and feel, the *skin*, of the poem. "Carefulness" helps to break down the wall. I wrote an essay called "Goatfoot, Milktongue, Twinbird," where I finally showed—to myself, I suppose; I wrote it to Robert Bly, whom I would like to persuade of the thought—that "technique" is not just technique. None of that Famous Writers School or MFA crap is what I'm talking about. That the feel of the poem in the mouth is the necessary prelude to magical thinking. But I said all that there. Anyway, I was into destroying myself, or evading myself, which is the same thing. After *The Yellow Room* I went into prose poems a lot. Then a lot into humor. In some ways I'm still there. Oh, I don't know where I am.

It seems to me that The Alligator Bride—*which is a selection of poems, of course—was a way of putting the past into the past. It closed a book. It was finished. It seems to me that you are saying that* The Yellow Room *is past also, and that you are getting it behind you, transcending it.*

Maybe. Look. Nobody has any right to talk about his own work. My low opinion of *The Yellow Room* is perfectly valueless. After all, I have every reason to have distorted views of everything. I do prefer *The Alligator Bride*. There are particular poems there—in the middle section, rewrites from *A Roof*, and in the last section the title poem, and "The Man in the Dead Machine"— which seem to be better than anything I've done since. But let the past be the past.

One thing that made The Yellow Room *distinct was that it was a whole book, a singular item. Do you see yourself doing something like that again?*

Yes, I do think so. Not in the same way. About two years ago, I started to write drafts, and to take notes, for a poem which I am calling *Building the House of Dying*. I suppose I have sixty or seventy pages. Maybe more. Stylistically, they are close to the new poem, "The Toy Bone." I mean, I guess they are closer to that than to the style of *The Yellow Room* or of *The Alligator Bride*. I don't know quite what form this will take. I think it will be a whole book. This book, as I think of it, will be *inclusive*—in the way that Galway talked about bringing your whole life to the poem. The structure that interests me is the juxtaposition of separate pieces, not detachable poems, but whole lumps, without transitions between them. I can call it ideogrammic—but I'm not sure that I want to make the comparison to Pound. Pound may make a one-page unit out of four or five different items. I mean that my units are a page or even several pages, complete in themselves, then gathering something to themselves by what comes after, and after that. These units would not be related to each other by chronology, or by lists, or by Monday-Tuesday-Wednesday sort of thing. Arrangement might seem random, but it wouldn't be. Sequential, but not orderly in a conventional way. More like the organization of "Song of Myself" than like the organization of the *Cantos*. In writing some prose pieces recently, like the review I did for you of Robert Bly, and the thing about baseball which I wrote last spring, I have used such a technique. Juxtaposition of whole parts, without transitions.

You have a feel for simultaneity.

I guess I reach toward it.

You might want to put all the pages on the wall and read them at the same time, if that were possible.

Yes, and since it isn't possible, you arrange them in the best possible way, and one of the criteria for "best" is that it's not obvious why you put them this way.

I do not mean this to be a narrow question, but critical terms like "vulnerability," and "fullness," and "openness . . ."

Those were not the critical terms I grew up with!

I know. But we use them as critical terms now. While you were talking about The Yellow Room, *I was remembering "The Toy Bone" which you read a little while ago, and it seems to me that the speaking voice in "The Toy Bone" is more vulnerable than the voice in* The Yellow Room.

I hope so. I think that one thing I've moved toward, *more or less* steadily, is vulnerability. With relapses, as I said. All the way from the carapace of *Exiles and Marriages* in 1955 to what I hope to be doing in *Building the House of Dying.* And of course when there are detours, they never present themselves as detours. They present themselves as "the shortest distance between two points."

Do you think it's possible, judging from your own work, to take "vulnerability" as a stance? Openness as a stance? To let these things become a carapace?

Absolutely! What a sophisticated question! It happens all the time. Jesus, sincerity is the biggest con there is. Every solution is a trap. I've fallen into that one, sometimes. There are many ways to fail, and the ways of failure group around each success, like systems of planets around each star. The illusion of vulnerability can be a guilt-making device: "Look how vulnerable I am, you creep!" I see this in poetry right now. Right now there is a good deal of pseudo-vulnerable poetry which is sentimental and hostile. It says, "*I* have the courage to be sentimental. Why don't *you*?" Bull shit. Sentimentality is narcissism. It is looking into the mirror and saying how wonderful I am to have these feelings, and to have them in public. Thereupon, this poem turns and licks itself all over, coos itself into sleep, smiling with the thought of its own beauty. It's enough to give vulnerability a bad name. When I associate it with sentimentality, I am talking about a perversion of vulnerability. Sentimentality is the opposite of true vulnerability; sentimentality is emotional dishonesty used to protect oneself from the harshness of the truth perceived. And on the other hand, to be vulnerable is to be open to that wounding perception. The sentimental man is the man closed to wounding. Paradoxically, one of his chief ways—at least among contemporary poets—of closing himself to the wounding is to tell us how wounded he is. So as "an emotional stance," as something chosen, as a kind of pose, I suppose it is sentimental. As a commitment or an engagement, vulnerability would be the attempt to walk through the woods without weapon or armor. The attempt *really* to do this. That would be a good thing. But it is not the only good thing. That is, some poetry which is invulnerable is very beautiful and fine. I think that Richard Wilbur is invulnerable. And beautiful. And fine.

In your Building the House of Dying, *is there a real house? Is that your ancestral house?*

Yes, there's a real house. But I don't really live there. I don't really own it. I might. It's the house in New Hampshire where I spent all my summers with my grandfather. I wrote a prose book about it, *String Too Short to Be Saved,* and I've written about it again and again in poems. I didn't think I'd ever live there. When I wrote the poem "Mount Kearsarge," I said "I will not rock on this porch/when I am old." Now it seems possible, suddenly. I am trying to buy the house. My great grandfather was the last person to buy it, in 1865. He farmed it, then his daughter's husband—my grandfather—farmed it. Now his daughter—my grandmother—is ninety-five, and dying. The house will have to be sold. The line in "Mount Kearsarge" spooks me out now. Does it mean that if I do buy it I will die, that I will never get old? I want to go there and live. I want to live a life of reflection and discovery through language. I want to write and read. I'm tired of teaching. I liked teaching for a long time. I remember Henry Moore saying that teaching was very good for him, the first ten years or so, when he said things he didn't know that he knew. When he started hearing his voice repeat things, he knew it was time to get out. Well, I hear myself repeat things.

Do you expect to write more criticism?

Lately I have been doing more. And I think it's been helpful to me, to get me back into poetry, out of this detour I've been in. To write about poetry from time to time can be a great help to a poet. You have to make yourself think things through. You find out you know things you didn't know you knew. So it's like teaching then. But it's more demanding. Also, I simply think that everyone should change his circumstances now and then. I've been moving toward this for a long time. I want to make my living by reading my poems aloud in public, and by writing books.

That's your connection with prose, mostly, isn't it? I mean, that it helps you write poems by providing you with an income?

Yes, but not only that. Making a living was my first excuse for writing prose. But now I know that it has other importances also. If I am very busy on a prose project, in some strange way it *frees* me to write poetry. I remember years ago when I was a Junior Fellow at Harvard, with all the free time in the world to do whatever I wanted, I got all freaked out about writing poetry— about whether I was any *good*, about whether I was writing *enough*. I remember Louis Simpson writing me at that time, and saying, in effect, that when I grew up and had to make a living, in the real world, I wouldn't have to think about being a poet all day long, and life would be easier. Times when I am working toward a prose deadline—writing about baseball, writing a Profile or something—I sneak away from this project to the glad island of poetry, with such relief, and with such a sense of escape. Pressure seems to open things up. Gertrude Stein parked at intersections in Paris, with the horns beeping like crazy, in order to take the top layer of her mind off, and get the writing started. Hart Crane wrote with Ravel's "Bolero" blasting in his ear, and a jug of white wine beside him, in order to get things to come out. In my case, I think that some sort of ongoing project—or just in general trying to live by my wits—takes away the top layer of my mind.

It's kind of unusual for poets to write prose to make money now. How did you get the idea?

Well, there are all these poets writing for *Sports Illustrated* now. Galway Kinnell once. Jim Harrison often. J. D. Reed. Dan Gerber. Tom Clark wants to be a sports writer. I think perhaps it will get more common in the next few years. I suppose I got the idea from Robert Graves. (Of course Englishmen had been doing it for centuries, and everybody on the Continent.) When I first came to Michigan, to teach, Graves came to read his poems. I remember saying to him that I envied him so much, writing all those different *kinds* of books, and making a living that way. I told him I wished I could do that. He looked me in the eye and asked me if I had ever tried. Well, that had never occurred to me! Of course I hadn't tried. So I tried. I sold some things, I did some poetry readings, and every time I made any money out of writing I would put it in a special savings account, and when I had enough saved up I would take time off from teaching. Really, that's what I've done all along. Now I think I'm at a point when perhaps I can take off from teaching entirely. Of course it's possible that I might go through life writing prose in order to have time to write poems, and in the end really be a better prose writer than a poet. Some friends think that *String Too Short to Be Saved* is better than any of my poems.

Do you like doing poetry readings?

Very much. I like performing. I like publishing my own work in that intimate way, catching people's eyes, feeling their response. Also, I learn things by going back over my own work. Every now and then I find a poem that I had lost. Recently I found "The Corner," which I think is good, but which is frightening. Reading it again was a new discovery.

Is that what you want a poem to do? To be a discovery? Do you have hopes for each poem in terms of its career as a psychic phenomenon?

I want it to open up, in the phrase you used earlier.

What is it that you want it to open up?

It is as if you were in a room, a familiar room. Suddenly you notice a door you never noticed before. You open it up, and there's a valley—acres and acres and acres. By the act of opening the door, you create the valley. In some poems, when you open the door you find another room with another door, and you open that and there is another room and so on. Or you find the skeletons. Writing poetry is revelation. Doing poetry readings, I find myself telling stories about how I wrote each poem, and telling them with great excitement, as if I were talking about how I trapped a pterodactyl. The pursuit of the strange creature, the chase, that is what is so exciting. Poetry is the *act* of writing poetry.

Is the poem itself trying to repeat the act of surprise?

Getting the poem right involves embodying the surprise, which is the act of writing it. Of course the act of the surprise is not complete until I have heard the right words. Poems can begin all sorts of ways. I've had poems begin with intense visual images. "The Man in the Dead Machine" began that way. Most poems begin with the sudden gift of words, just winging into the head. And a few poems begin out of conversation. "The Toy Bone" began that way. I was talking with a friend, a scientist who loves poetry, a man called Chia-Shun Yih. I was telling him about the bone which I found in the attic, and the things which it reminded me of. The memory brought all sorts of things with it. I had to go back and find out, in my imagination, what it was in the attic that I was finding, and what that room was really like, and what I did in it. Such strange things happened! When the poem was almost finished, I went back to that house, where my mother lives alone now. Thinking about that poem, I followed a sort of track, went upstairs, turned a corner, opened the door—a real door, this time—walked into a closet of my old bedroom, put my hand up to a shelf, and pulled down the record of Connie Boswell singing "The Kerry Dancers." For various reasons, I am sure that I cannot have touched that record for thirty years. Something in me knew where it was. Remembered.

Take a step back from this poem, or from any poem. You've been describing what you want a poem to do for you. What about the reader?

The act of reading the poem, if the words are right, will embody the surprise of the act of writing it. I believe that the way out and the way in resemble each other. The act of writing a poem and the act of reading a poem resemble each other in structure. A little series of explosions of understanding occur in the act of reading. This idea presupposes that the reader and the writer share a great deal. I'm happy to make that presupposition. Also, the idea presupposes and lends weight to the idea that the poem can happen—poetry can happen—because of collaboration between the "adult" brain and "infant" brain in the poet (the brain "adult" in the sense that it knows how to read). We can get very sophisticated about reading, and the more we do so the better. Sophisticated is not to say intellectual. The more we read poems, the better we are able to read any single poem. But the universality comes about not because of the act of reading but because the motions of the poem which release the mind into its magic and infantile state bring us to a level of shared experience where we are more like each other than we are in adult lives.

When I said "fullness" earlier, and talked about "simultaneity," maybe I meant that joining together of the reader and the writer.

Making oneness. The *synthetic*.

Yes. The synthetic. I feel in "The Toy Bone" the making one of the adult and the infant mind. Not that they are just there together. *I didn't want to say that. That's why I didn't want to say simultaneity. They have been melded . . .*

So they make a new other thing, I hope.

Which is maybe the real thing we are.

Another thing that makes me think of (this is another subject, sort of, but you'll see how I got here): I look at the works of the great poets on the bookshelves, *so* thick; in how many pages of that thickness does anything like what we are ultimately looking for really happen? Maybe we live a whole lifetime for a total of five minutes, of moments of coming-together. How many minutes in Robert Frost's life were really the making of metaphor?

What you were saying a minute ago makes me think of something. I half believe—maybe more than half—that poetry is our way of creating wholeness and continuity for our times, that when the poem really works, the individual life will continue.

We have a continuity with the past. We attempt continuity with a nebulous future. That's why the artist's daydream about posterity and fame has its validity, its seriousness. My utopian optimism suggests that we write toward a change of human kind, that we write *toward* an evolutionary leap, that we write with that part of ourselves which wishes not to die, as a race, but to survive. Poetry leads to survival. Oh, there is a poetry of destructiveness, heaven knows. The generation of Jarrell and Lowell had so much destruction in it. And goodness knows, if we are going to talk about vulnerability and openness, we are talking about *dangers*. But it was dangerous to come down out of the trees, it was dangerous to learn how to use fire; and these acts, dangerous as they were, were necessary to survival.

The survival you speak of is dependent on metamorphosis or change?

Yes. And poetry is the advance guard of that change.

The instrument and cause, or at least instrument?

I don't think it's a cause. I think it is an instrument. I think it is an indicator. A gnomon. But it doesn't *show* us the way, so much as it exemplifies, in fragments and in moments, that unification which *is* the way—and the place we must reach, the country we must move to and live in.

Poem Mentioned in this Interview

The Toy Bone

Looking through boxes
in the attic of my mother's house in Hamden,
I find a model airplane, snapshots
of a dog wearing baby clothes,
a catcher's mitt—the oiled
pocket eaten
by mice—and I discover
the toy bone, the familiar
smell of it.

I sat alone each day
after school, in the living room
of my parents' house in Hamden, ten
years old, eating
slices of plain white bread.
I listened to the record, Connie
Boswell singing
again and again, her voice
turning like a heel, "The Kerry Dancers,"
and I knew she was crippled, and sang
from a wheelchair. I played
with Tommy, my red-and-white
Shetland collie, throwing
his toy bone
into the air and catching it, or letting it fall,
while he watched me

with intent, curious eyes.
I was happy
in the room dark with the shades drawn.

And now, climbing the attic stairs,
I pause for breath, the way
my father used to.

Larkin and Larkinism

Last summer the BBC sent me Philip Larkin's new anthology—*The Oxford Book of Twentieth Century English Verse*—and asked me to do a talk about it. I guess they thought an American opinion might be useful. Well, I read it straight through, and I hated it. I wrote a talk which sputtered, and raged, and sagged into total incoherence. I showed it to the BBC anyway. They allowed as how it wasn't much good. They said that, to you listening, it would just sound like another American being snotty about English poetry. I had to agree. So I'm trying again.

The thing is, I'm *not* just another American being snotty about English poetry. I'm a damned *Anglophile*, a mid-Atlantic type. For *years*, I've been telling Englishmen about American poetry, and Americans about English poetry. Nationalistic hostilities—all those clichés on both sides of the Atlantic—annoy the hell out of me. For instance, America is *full* of people who repeat derogatory clichés about English poetry, and who couldn't tell Empsonian terza rima from a Liverpool pop lyric. I want to shake these people by their shoulders. "The

---

"Larkin and Larkinism" was brodcast on the BBC in 1974, and addressed to English listeners.

Revolution is over!" I tell them, in confidence. "The British troops surrendered and went home! The Hessians too! We can have our own literature now! We have these new writers: Hawthorne, Melville, Emerson, Thoreau, Whitman. We don't *have* to hate the English any more!" And I try to get these people to read Geoffrey Hill or Ted Hughes—or Philip Larkin, for that matter.

Then this anthology comes along and confirms everybody's worst prejudices against English poetry of the twentieth century. I feel as if I were the public relations officer for the Acme Cement Company; I've spent all day extolling the virtues of Acme Cement to a committee of contractors, pointing at a poured concrete edifice in front of us—and then suddenly the whole building falls apart, crumbles, sags, and crashes into rubble in front of our eyes.

Well, "Heh heh," I say, "What do you know about that? . . . "

Despite the excellence of much current poetry in England, there's a loose series of ideas which undercut the English poetic scene. It's a bad kit of destructive conventions, about poetry, and about the making of poetry. These "social instructions," as I'll call them, call for a poetry which is modest, which is to say trivial, and unpretentious, which is to say incompetent. And that's only the beginning. When these sad doctrines are promulgated abroad—maybe in the TLS, maybe in this Oxford Anthology—English poetry looks like a province of imbeciles and cretins.

These doctrines or instructions or ideas or conventions I lump together as "Larkinism." They antedate Philip Larkin and they exist in people who don't resemble him otherwise, but he deserves the term, because

I find the poetry of these conventions neatly gathered in this anthology, by Philip Larkin.

Of course when he writes poetry, Philip Larkin is no Larkinist. When he writes his poems, Larkin brings to them an accumulated skill, delicate and fully articulate, an easy movement, and intricate sensitive feeling. He is also grandly ambitious, whether he admits it or not. A poem like "The Whitsun Weddings"—you couldn't make a thing like that unless you were willing to risk everything. And risk is a huge element in Larkin's poems. Listen again to an old and familiar poem, "Coming":

> On longer evenings,
> Light, chill and yellow,
> Bathes the serene
> Foreheads of houses.
> A thrush sings,
> Laurel-surrounded
> In the deep bare garden,
> Its fresh-peeled voice
> Astonishing the brickwork.
> It will be spring soon,
> It will be spring soon—
> And I, whose childhood
> Is a forgotten boredom,
> Feel like a child
> Who comes on a scene
> Of adult reconciling,
> And can understand nothing
> But the unusual laughter,
> And starts to be happy.

How open he is, how audacious, how intelligent, how beautiful. This poem can survive even an American accent, I believe. Larkin comes so close to sentimentality, to banality, as close as you can come, but he does *not* slip over into the narcissism that would be so tempting. Accurate observation wins through. He cares enough for poetry to make it right. What a master he is.

And yet Larkin is not much read in the United States, at this time. I'm sure in the *long* run everybody will acknowledge his mastery. But at the moment, the American convention demands novelty in poetry. There is a rhetoric of change, which cannot accept Larkin because he sounds old fashioned. Or which *does* accept him as a curiosity, which is worse, accepts him as an eccentric occasion for nostalgia—as one might look upon a recently built traction engine, or a musical group which modeled itself on Louis Armstrong's Hot Five.

I digress about this American provinciality, because I think it's exactly parallel to Larkinism. Larkinism finds *all* innovation distasteful, and what is more amazing, it looks at an ancient technique like free verse and finds it innovative and therefore out of bounds. Kingsley Amis—that arch Larkinist—took up the attack in the *Observer* last September, with a conservatism that told us what it *wouldn't* do. In the same series, spokesmen for ballet and theatre were energetic and excited with what they were *doing* and were *going* to do. In England, theater—with its energy, its vast competence, and its originality—could be a model for all arts everywhere. But Larkinism is all *negative* energy: we will *not* be pretentious, we will *not* be obscure, we will *not* be novel, we will *not* take ourselves seriously.

I think about Mario, who lost out to the Magician, in Thomas Mann's novella, because willing the negative makes you concentrate on the proposition that you detest. Instead, you've got to find out what you're for, and concentrate on *it*.

The idea that you shouldn't take yourself seriously offends me more than anything.

Yes, I really said that.

But before you tell your friends what you heard the American say on the wireless, and how you admire Americans for their bumptious naivety, their energy, their love of bright colors, and their sense of rhythm—before you start condescending to me, think of what your condescension *means*. If you don't "take yourself seriously," do you mean to limp giggling into the grave and nothing more? Oh, it reminds me of *high school*, years ago, and all the girls who chewed gum and wore saddle shoes and told me I took myself too seriously.

Watching John Betjeman on BBC TV last autumn, I kept thinking of those gum chewers and saddle shoe wearers. The show was questions and answers, and the laureate found *all* the questions uniformly charming, and answered most of them by saying that, after all, the most important thing was not to take yourself seriously, wasn't it?

And in a dream-vision I saw the great English poets sitting in front of a gigantic television set in Paradise, watching John Betjeman giving forth this wisdom. "Oh, yes," said John Keats, "as I frequently said in my letters, not to mention my poems, the greatest thing for the poet is never to take life and death as if they mattered."

William Blake took his thumb out of his mouth and continued, "Yes, all of us great English poets are distinguished by our frivolity."

Yeats looked up from the dinner table where he sat with Landor and with Donne. "Irish, too," he said. "We chuckle a lot, to show that we are not pretentious."

You see, I think that Larkinism is *not* a great old English tradition, not at all. I think it is recent, and I think it derives from two apparently opposite social stances. One is the giggly side of Bloomsbury, desperate never to commit the *gaffe* of solemnity. The other is the plain-fellow, good-chap side of the followers of Dr. Leavis, terrified that commitment to an *art* will make them look like a Sitwell. Wine-sippers and Nescafé-drinkers come together in the self-deprecating, suicidal modesty of Larkinism.

It is modesty that distinguishes Larkinism, dreadful old modesty. Negative energy attacks ambition, calling it pretention. Short views and small holdings are praised not for their competence, but for their shortness and smallness.

So this anthology is *full* of modest poems.

Since neither modesty nor shortness nor smallness characterize the great poets, you would think that a Larkinist anthology would be hard on Yeats and Eliot and Hardy. But no. Larkin's Oxford book deals well with the great departed. It's with the incompetent departed, and the incompetent living, that Larkinism really shows itself. Of the better English poets now living, only one is represented by a selection which is copious and just. And that is the group of poems by Philip Larkin.

Ted Hughes appears with only five poems, fewer than the incompetent exercises of Roy Fuller, with his tin ear and his meretricious metaphors. And then there is . . .

But one could go on listing injustices forever, and besides, I will begin to sputter and to rage again.

Suffice it to say that Geoffrey Hill, who is at least as good as Larkin or as Hughes, is represented by one twenty-year-old poem, published while he was an undergraduate, which is sixteen lines long.

And the sins of inclusion overwhelm the sins of exclusion. To leave out the likes of Seamus Heaney, Tom Raworth, Lee Harwood, George MacKay Brown, Tom

Pickard and Richard Murphy—that is bad enough. The contemptuous *in*clusion of one or two inferior poems by superior poets—like Hill, like Jon Silkin—is worse.

And worst of all is the canonization of incompetence. For instance, here are eight and one-half pages of drivel by Sir John Squire; here are nine pages of a doggerel argument between Alex Comfort and George Orwell; and hundreds of pages of bad minor verse, the elephant's graveyard of TLS poems, poems by essayists, poems by scientists, and all too few poems by poets.

I exaggerate.

But I don't exaggerate much.

Larkinism chooses poems as if to enshrine provinciality, as if whatever was *English*—or almost, what *seems* English to foreigners—is to be celebrated. The result is an insularity which looks as artificial as a travel poster—hundreds of poems about cats and dogs, cheerfully racist poems making fun of the wogs, poems ridiculing homosexuals and modern art. And it is typical both of the clichéd technique of this poetry, and of its flog-'em hang-'em politics, that the most popular rhyme unites "beauty" with "duty."

Of course it's possible to write poems which are at once competent and offensive, which advocate deplorable ideas with elegance and wit. But when the Larkinist affirms Englishness, incompetence becomes the Englishman's birthright. I suppose it is an homage to "amateurism." But the players are better players than the gentlemen, gentlemen.

If one took this anthology as representative, one would have to conclude that the twentieth-century English versifier cannot write verse, cannot make meter without missing the beat, cannot make metaphors without comic and inadvertent juxtaposition. Even the rhyming is appalling. One poet refers to " . . . the other chap/Whom in jail you'd like to clap . . . " Cliché abounds, with its procession of moribund metaphors. If there is a "gulf," it "yawns," and it cannot be "bridged."

Originality and competence apparently seem pretentious to the Larkinist. I suppose they might indicate that you took poetry seriously. Or even took yourself seriously.

But there is no way to be good except by trying to be great.

When the poetry editor of a leading weekly announces that poetry is a modest art—and says this in the country of Wordsworth, and in the city of Shakespeare—we are in trouble. We are in trouble when the manners of the schoolyard intrude upon the practice of an art. For surely incompetence and cliché become virtues only because we learn in school never to expose ourselves to possible ridicule. Amateurism and modesty is self-defense, and Larkinism trivializes art, for fear of social ridicule.

Geoffrey Hill's Poems

English poetry in the twentieth century is Thomas Hardy, D. H. Lawrence, and Geoffrey Hill. When in the future flustered doctoral candidates confuse Auden with Austin; when Larkin becomes a small figure in the shadow of Hardy; when we no longer condescend to Irish and Scots by calling them English, Geoffrey Hill will remain the monumental English poet of the latter twentieth century.

Monumental he is, and marmoreal as well. In recent months, he has published devotional sonnets in English magazines. *Devotional sonnets*? Yes, and they have a weight, a serious sonority, unlike other English poems since the seventeenth century.

If he were an American poet, he would be unspeakably bad. Fortunately he is English. Only by acknowledging the separateness of English and American literature—like the continents they may drift slowly; but like the continents, there is an ocean between—can we begin to read Geoffrey Hill.

It is ironic that American poets pointed Hill in the direction of his Englishness. He began to write in the late forties and early fifties, a bad patch in English poetry. He may have learned something from Dylan Thomas. He loved the mellifluousness, scored into

"Genesis," which he has come to detest; it's no matter; we all hate our early poems, and we hate most the ones which were praised the most; these are the poems about which we heard the words we daydreamed we would hear, and therefore we despise the poems—and probably the people who spoke the words.

He learned more from the fierce control of Allen Tate; from Tate above all—an American performing to Mr. Eliot's Reading List.

Perhaps Americans Geoffrey Hill's age, reacting against their fathers, have found it difficult to read poems by this Englishman for whom Tate was not a father but an exotic alien, in love with dangerous syllables and rugged syntax.

Still, the tardiness of American response is sordid. When *For the Unfallen* appeared in England sixteen years ago, Dufour Editions imported some copies; I never saw it in a bookstore. For two decades, Hill has been the subject of a small cult in this country, probably about the size of Manson's family. At last Houghton Mifflin has published this assemblage of Hill's three English books; after *For the Unfallen* came *King Log* and most recently *Mercian Hymns*; together they make *Somewhere Is Such a Kingdom*.

Bound up with them, alas, is an introduction by Harold Bloom. It is as if the publisher, guilty about the Promethean gift of a great poem to American readers, at the last moment decided to erect a barrier. Houghton Mifflin might as well have electrified the entire edition. Attempting to read Geoffrey Hill through the fog of Harold Bloom is like attending a Matisse exhibition wearing mud-colored Foster Grants. Bloom admires Hill because Hill is difficult.

Therefore must we admire Bloom *more*, because Bloom is *more* difficult?

Bloom's name on the jacket will turn a thousand readers away. *Please* don't turn away because of Bloom. Buy the book, read Hill, and ignore Bloom. Better still, tear the introduction out of the book and return it to Houghton Mifflin.

Geoffrey Hill began writing poems in his native village in the south of England, walking in the fields and grumbling vowels at the stones. After a few years at Oxford, he headed north for a job teaching at Leeds, vastly separated from cozy London and the literary life.

The best contemporary English poets after Hill live in a village outside Bristol, in Hull, in a Yorkshire town, in Cornwall and Devon, in Texas, in California. The virtues of a capital have been wrecked by the vices of chumminess. Capital cities are no longer useful to poets.

Hill writes packed, balanced sentences. No one makes a tighter line, or, in the prose poems of *Mercian Hymns*, a sentence more dense with variety, or more unified by strenuous syntax. He loads every rift with ore.

Early Hill is "beautiful," by which I mean that it can be ingratiating. I may as well quote from "Genesis," which is the one poem of Hill's which people remember, if they remember one poem by Hill.

> And by Christ's blood are men made free
> Though in close shrouds their bodies lie
> Under the rough pelt of the sea.

One is permitted, I think, to suspect that the young poet cares less about Christ's blood than he cares for the sound "Christ's blood" makes: the rhythmical figure of the first two lines—a softer pair of syllables, followed by a louder pair—*almost* repeats itself in the third line; but *no*, there is a medial inversion turning on "pelt," causing a gorgeous pause between "rough" and "pelt"—which is the holiday our tongue always longed for.

In slightly later work, Hill plays more obviously with syntax, or with the relationship of line to syntax, than he does with sound; sound is there, brilliantly there, but it calls no attention to itself. Here Hill taxes Orpheus, poet as Narcissus (from "Orpheus and Eurydice"):

> Love goes, carrying compassion
> To the rawly difficult;
> His countenance, his hands' motion
> Serene even to a fault.

" . . . a fault" indeed. Later still, the verse is more crabbed, and the meditation similar in its ambivalence. He continues his assault on the controlling and verbal mind (from "Three Baroque Meditations"):

> Do words make up the majesty
> Of man, and his justice
> Between the stones and the void?

If they do—and they may—it goes hard with us. After the abstraction, the pain follows, more intimate now:

> An owl plunges to its tryst
> With a field-mouse in the sharp night.
> My fire squeals and lies still.

Then comes the bewildering about face of *Mercian Hymns*. Reading *Somewhere Is Such a Kingdom* you move from the line of *King Log* ("My fire squeals and lies still") to the paragraph of King Offa:

> King of the perennial holly-groves, the riven sandstone;
> overlord of the M5: architect of the historic rampart
> and ditch, the citadel at Tamworth, the summer hermitage

in Holy Cross: guardian of the Welsh Bridge and the
Iron Bridge: contractor to the desirable new estates:
saltmaster: money changer: commissioner for oathes:
"I liked that," said Offa, "sing it again."

Perhaps a man gifted with the English line, whose great-
est skill is to break the English sentence (I paraphrase
Frost) over the English line, who enjambs and meters
with unmatched skill—maybe he needs to discover if he
can discard the weapons he has forged for decades, and
do battle with bare hands, and survive; even triumph.

"Bare hands" is exaggeration. Look at the grammat-
ical changes rung in only the first paragraph of *Mercian
Hymns*. Hill allows himself two notes, the noun and the
prepositional phrase, and he finds twelve octaves be-
tween his notes.

Subject matter is similar to earlier work, with suffer-
ing and vanity braided together, but the sound is new,
and when a poet makes a new sound, he speaks from a
part of body and of soul that has been silent before.
New sound extends the limits of diction; or maybe it
only changes the territory delimited. No matter, the
novelty (for Hill) is sufficient: anachronism allows Hill's
politics to speak. And the form of prose (with an irony
frequently encountered when making poetry) allows
Hill's sound to be more gorgeous than it has been since
"Genesis," gorgeous without being ingratiating.

Tracks of ancient occupation. Frail ironworks rusting
in the thorn-thicket. Hearthstone; charred lullabyes,
A solitary axe-blow that is the echo of a lost sound.

Tumult recedes as though into the long rain. Groves of
legendary holly; silverdark the ridged gleam.

Intone this to the fields of England, and the stones will
rise and follow you.

More Questions

In 1975, Alberta Turner sent out a questionnaire about poetic composition, asking poets to answer her questions by using one poem as an example. I wrote a letter in answer, from which I have excerpted the following pages. This is the poem about which I wrote.

The Town of Hill

Back of the dam, under
a flat pad

of water, church
bells ring

in the ears of lilies,
a child's swing

curls in the current
of a yard, horned

pout sleep
in a green

mailbox, and
a boy walks

from a screened
porch beneath

the man-shaped
leaves of an oak

down the street looking
at the town

of Hill that water
covered forty

years ago,
and the screen

door shuts
under dream water.

How did the poem start?

The poem started with a few notes taken when I visited
my old family farm in New Hampshire, perhaps in the
summer of 1970 or '71. Hill is a town in New Hampshire.
There was an old town, flooded for a flood-control
project—and now there is a new town. When I was a
kid, I visited the old town shortly before everything
was removed from it. (Not everything was removed. But
the people were, and moveable houses were.) In '70 or
'71 I remembered the town, and took a few notes about
a town under water.

What changes did the poem go through?

I cannot really answer this. It went through three
years of intensive work, with lots and lots of changes.
I've got all of the copies of it somewhere or other. It

was shorter to begin with, then it was longer than it is now. What is the middle was once the ending. I kept thinking I had finished it. I would work on it one morning, feel enthusiastic, tell someone how good it was, and a day or two later I would see that it was not. I showed it to Jane Kenyon and to Greg Orr (with whom I've been working a lot, the last three years) over and over again. I sent various versions of it to various friends, including Stuart Friebert at one point. I cannot remember right now what he said about it, but I think I took some help from him.

It was a poem which went back to an earlier style. I don't think it looks much like the other poems, but it is a poem that is greatly dependent on, and interested in, its own sound. It is Goatfoot and Milktongue—and probably more Milktongue than Goatfoot. And I think that's what it secretly is about. About life before birth even or perhaps very early on after birth. But I'm not *sure* what it is secretly about, not yet. That usually takes me a few years. I mean, a few years after it's finished.

It arrived at its present state about a year ago. Lately, when I read it, I begin to wonder about one or two words in it, so it may go through some more changes. And of course in the meantime I have no idea whether it's any good or not. I mean, I hope it is, I have real hopes for it sometimes, but I don't *really* know. I do "really" know, I think, about a few poems, as recent as eight years old, or as old as twenty-five years. I know about a lot of them that they are no good. I think I know about a few of them that they are good. But this one is far too new for that kind of knowledge.

What techniques did you consciously use?

None. I mean, I am constantly aware of assonance, of

syntax, etc. But I don't consciously use any principles of technique. Come to think of it, I don't know what "principles of technique" would really mean. Unless it meant something like meter, and this poem is not metrical.

Whom did you visualize as your reader?

Robert Bly, Galway Kinnell, Jane Kenyon, Gregory Orr, Louis Simpson, and Thom Gunn.

Can the poem be paraphrased?

Not really. That is, of course, one could substitute prose for the poetry, simply using Thesaurus "synonyms" for each of the words. But a paraphrase usually involves the translation of the irrational into the rational—if there *is* anything irrational—and in this poem, I don't think that the time-switch could be paraphrased *out*. Therefore, the mystery which exists in the plot would not be translated. Of course, the sound would be lost, the images manhandled, and other usual effects of paraphrase would indeed succeed.

How does this poem differ from earlier poems of yours?

I've already said that I can't tell how it differs in quality. In theme, I think perhaps it is part of a return to the past, and a re-examination of the past, which I have talked about earlier, but which this poem may well try to be deeper at. In technique, as I explained before, it is in one way a reversion to an earlier technique. When I began this poem, I had been spending a certain amount of time writing prose poems, in which attention to Goatfoot and Milktongue was minimal. Plot was important. Some logopoeia, some phanopoeia, but damned little melopoeia. And I was yearning for the old mouth-feel.

Was this poem initiated by free-association, by means of an epigraph, by answering the needs of an occasion, by deciding on a theme and seeking to embody it, by reaction to a strong emotion, by other means?

It began as a few words, connected with the town itself. And I felt that there was something to pursue, some quarry to be hunted, if I pursued the implications of these words in this rhythm.

When you were writing the poem, did you imagine any particular person or persons listening to it or arguing with it? If so, who?

Frequently, in late stages of revision, which is to say maybe the last two years of work on a poem, I argue with my friends about it when they are not there. They include the people I visualized above as the reader.

How many drafts did the poem go through?

Fifty or sixty.

What intervals of time elapsed between the drafts?

Sometimes I would do a draft a day, or perhaps 3 or 4 pages in one day. Other times I would not work on it for a month.

Did the poem shrink or expand?

It shrank and it expanded.

Did the structure change? How?

The structure changed. I didn't know how to end it. The part about the "man-shaped leaves. . ." was the ending for some time. Other things that ended it have now disappeared.

The theme? How?

I don't really know what the theme is.

The tone? How?

I don't think the tone changed.

Which lines remained unchanged? Why?

The early lines describing the town under water became set fairly early, probably within the first two or three months of writing it, and never changed, or changed very little. Because they were fixed. Because they were almost the *given.*

Of those lines which changed, did the changes fall more in the area of rhythm, sound, imagery, denotation, connotation, other? Why?

Connotation and sound.

On what principle or principles did you lineate the poem? Are alternative lineations possible?

Alternative lineations are possible, but this is the best one I can arrive at for the sound by itself—which is one separate thing; the sound as reinforcing sense, or enforcing sense for the first time—but which can exist only if the first conditions are met. Sound as rock.

What rhythmical principle did you use? Iambic, accentual, syllabic, speech cadence, the cadence of idea groups, the cadence of a particular emotion, the cadence of a bodily rhythm, other?

I didn't think of any rhythmical principle. I never do. That is, iambic is *not* a rhythmical principle! As many rhythms are possible in iambic as are in free verse, as syllabic, accentual, etc.

On what principle or principles did you use sound repetition (end or internal): exact rhyme, assonance, alliteration, consonance, onomatopoeia, phonetic intensives, other?

No principles for assonance, etc. Just delight, excitement, etc.

Would you prefer this poem to be read silently, aloud, to musical accompaniment?

I would prefer this poem to be read aloud, *by me.*

On what principles did you use the metaphorical process (conventional metaphor, simile, symbol, etc.; surrealism; or literal statement or details implying metaphor)? Or did you consciously avoid metaphor? Or did you unconsciously achieve metaphor by using literal details in such a way that they implied metaphor?

About the principles of metaphor and so on. I come to realize that most of these questions embarrass me because I don't think I'm the one to answer them. I think that they *imply* that I know more about my poem than somebody else. I don't think I do. I think that authors have in fact a considerable reason to lie to themselves about what they do and why they do what they do. So I don't trust what they say. And I apply these principles of distrust to myself.

I didn't consciously apply any of these principles.

Did you consciously avoid or seek abstract language, esoteric language, "poetic" diction, or any other specific kind or mannerism of diction?

I do have preconscious standards about rhythms, and about diction. These preconscious standards derive from my love of Ezra Pound, Keats, and great poets.

Did you consciously avoid or seek any pattern or mannerism of sentence structure, such as questions, imperatives, direct address, series, parenthetical expressions, fragments, other?

Toward the end, I became aware that I was writing a single sentence, and became interested in the problem of my syntax. But only after I was doing it.

On what principles did you use reference and allusion: conventional historical and literary reference and allusion, personal reference and allusion recognizable by only a small group of friends or fellow poets, contemporary reference and allusion recognizable by the public at large, other?

No reference or allusion. I know people don't know what a "horned pout" is, but I don't care.

By what principles did you structure the poem? A familiar prose structure such as cause and effect, thesis-amplification, question-answer, or a psychological order as in dreams of free-association? Other?

Improvisation. I kept changing the organization of things. Certainly the organization is in some sense psychological. Certainly the various orders were not thought out ahead of time, but improvised, looked at, rejected, tried again.

Did you consciously avoid or seek an open-ended conclusion, a firmly conclusive ending, a climactic or anti-climactic ending, other?

I sought a conclusive ending, but not a conclusive ending intellectually, really a conclusive ending rhythmically, and in sound. I wonder now that I picked the word "dream" for its assonance, and am stuck with it as intellectual fingerpointing!

Is the persona in the poem yourself, a part of yourself, other? Why did you use this persona?

The persona is always me. Except that a poem is not a person. And, therefore, I'm rejecting the question.

How did you use cliché in writing this poem? Avoid it altogether, incorporate recognizable cliché phrases with a new twist, exaggerate and so satirize clichés, other?

I did not use cliché in writing this poem deliberately. If there are clichés in this poem, they are the fault of my wicked self.

By what principles did you appeal to the reader's eye in arranging the poem on the page? Or did you make no conscious attempt to appeal to his eye?

Appeal to the eye? As it happened, the poem began to make this spacey, skinny thing, and I liked that. But I did not look forward to it.

How would you describe the tone of this poem? Nostalgic, satiric, reflective, ambivalent, other? What factors most conspicuously create this tone? Did you create it deliberately?

I cannot describe the tone particularly. The poem is to a degree nostalgic. The poem seems to me also somehow or other runic. But maybe I flatter it.

If it cannot be paraphrased by a prose statement, why not?

If it cannot be paraphrased, it simply cannot be paraphrased. Why do I have to give a reason? Earlier, perhaps I answered this, when I said that you could only paraphrase the irrational by another parallel irrationality, or some such thing. That is, I don't think you can explain it *away* in rational terms.

If a person who had had no experience with poetry written since World War II were confused by this poem, what steps would you take to help him read it?

If a person had no experience, I wouldn't attempt to help him read this poem. I would try to help him to read poetry. I would tell him, for instance, that he should not ask for a poem to do any particular thing. I would ask him to relax and listen and float. I would ask him to allow himself to associate. I would ask him—as I would ask anyone about any poems—not to translate but to listen. Most people read poems as if they were reading French badly, translating it into English as they went. To read the poem, you must *stop* paraphrasing, stop "thinking" in the conventional way, and do some receiving instead.

Finally, let me say that the more I see this poem, the more I come to doubt it. I think it is possible that by striving to go back to an early style, the really mouthy style, I have limited it in some way or other. Robert Bly keeps saying that it's what is behind that screen door that is really interesting. I think maybe the other poems—the ones I'm writing now in looser, longer lines, with repetitive rhythms—maybe these poems are what is behind the screen door.

Still More Notes on Poetry

THE POETRY READING

Anne Sexton's column in *American Poetry Review* —"The Freak Show"—attacks poetry readings because poets become freaks for the audience.

She mentions that I approve of readings as a way of "living by your wits." Yes, when you need the money, the poetry reading is there to be done; it's a way for a poet to make money without pretending to be something besides a poet. But for many poets, readings have become essential—for reasons besides making a living.

For many poets, readings have become the primary form of publication. Reading is a making-public, an utterance, which is far more immediate than any other form. If you publish a poem in a magazine, you wait six months to a year for it to come out, and then you may get a letter or two. No more than that. If you publish a book, you get a few reviews a year after publication. Two years after you were done with the manuscript, probably. Publication is like talking to yourself in a large, empty room.

If by some imperial decree we had to make a choice between reading aloud and publishing books, who would choose those tiny little volumes—all exactly like each other—in preference to the intense, variable, chancey, weird confrontation of your body-and-voice with the gathering of strange faces, the people out there?

Well, a number of people would. But I would choose the reading-aloud, and so would many others.

Years ago, publications like *Time* used to lament that "poetry has lost its audience," as if there had been some golden age a decade or two past when *Time* editors sat in their cabanas reading Trumbull Stickney. When the *Time* hack wrote "audience," he was being metaphorical, albeit unwittingly metaphorical; he did not consider poems audible. But now poems are audible constantly, from coast to coast, and poets are visible, and poetry has found its audience: rows and rows of people hearing the words and watching the gestures.

The poet reads, or croons, or sings; flaps arms, dances, weeps, tells jokes; solemn or hilarious, frightened or confident or both; making the wholly private act of writing the poem into the wholly public act of reading or performing the poem, with the energy created by this conflict, this tension of opposites.

Or sometimes—I forgot to say—the poet is boring, fatuous, stupid, obscene, drunk, paranoiac, incompetent, or inaudible.

But when the poet reads well, the gain for poetry is considerable. For the poet, there is the sense that people are really there. The audience responds more tangibly than a letter or a book review. Yeats writes somewhere about feeling discouraged, but finding when he read in a village a young man who carried a battered and loved copy of Yeats's poems with him.

More important, the act of reading is the poet's act of

truly publishing his poem—as the syllables waver on the air from poet to listener, and the faces change as the syllables reach them: as the faces laugh and weep, change color, or look away; as eyes flash up, or eyes drop.

And when we hear a poet read, whom we love, how touched and moved we are, to hear the voice itself pronounce the words we already know.

One more piece of praise for readings: many poets find that readings help their writing. Readings may help because praise helps; the bottomless pit can have a moment's illusion of fulfillment. Or because the isolation of the road helps; Galway Kinnell did much of his work on *The Book of Nightmares* in motels, reading incessantly because he was working to get himself out of debt. Or because of critical feedback which seems to come from the faces, and which at least comes from the situation: reading a new poem aloud, you feel a soft patch when you speak it; your foot makes the rotten ice creak.

Anne Sexton wrote that the visiting poet was a freak, a monster for the students and teachers to observe from a safe distance, and to laugh at.

I agree, and I think it is useful and correct, this freakishness. And the distance is a practical necessity.

Poetry embodies the *whole* of the emotional life, the many-angled horror and ecstasy, the hate and the love *together*. Ordinary social behavior—the students' and the teachers', and the poets' own—cannot embody this, or at least not consistently. Man has not evolved to this condition, or created the society in which this condition is possible.

But poetry does it. Therefore the poet does it when

he is making the poem. Making poems is not the poet's whole life. He eats breakfast, he reads the newspaper, he grumbles at the weather. But when the poet inhabits his poem by reading it, he becomes the *carrier* of this power.

Poetry has the power to wipe out the fall of man—for a moment—and to embody the unity of being possible to man if he superadds to his rational, fallen consciousness his prelapsarian and metaphorical intuition.

In the poem the poet becomes a freak—but a freak through his absolute health. He is almost a mutant. In fact, he may *be* a mutant. Poetry shows the direction in which it is possible that man can evolve, past the state of civilization.

So the poet's freakishness is wholly serious. The nervous response of the audience—insuring its separation by its giggles—pays tribute to the power of the example.

POEMS ALOUD ONCE MORE

For years, we have had LP's of poets' voices—from Spoken Arts (most monumentally the eighteen-volume set of American poets), from Caedmon, from Folkways, and from smaller sources. For that matter, poets as far back as Tennyson and Browning recorded wax records; granted that the quality of recording, with the older poets, makes "The Charge of the Light Brigade" sound like "Dueling Coffee Grinders." Still, we have some sense of voice, some sense of intonation, some sense of tone. And though we have little Joyce on record, what we have is priceless. Yeats's recordings are disappointing (in one of the grossest clerical errors of modern archivery, a BBC employee destroyed hours of Yeats preserved on wax, during the Second World War) but we hear the quaver and the croon.

But these records are merely reproductions of a man reading, like the film of a play. They are not a performance in which the performer connects with the intimate and exact nature of his performance. He does not use the microphone.

There *are* poets and writers, especially in England, who have made good use of radio. They tell us that the microphone—or to be more exact the radio in the listener's living room—is a special form of publication, and it requires special attention. If you address a microphone as if you were addressing a room full of listeners, you sound pompous. Gesture and clothing and eye contact, muscles and scowls, combine on the platform with the voice to make a possible whole. Print one part only—either eyebrow or voice—and you make a monster. Nothing sounds so false, to the ear in its living room, alone with its radio, as the public manners of a lecture platform.

(Exception can be live recording, where the response of the audience—its coughs, its laughter, its wiggles, and its applause—bodies itself to the ear, and the listener intuits the bodily presence of the reader on the platform.)

I suppose the emergence of a cassette public, which is a radio public which schedules its own programs, derives from the growth of the public for poetry readings. But only when poets begin to understand that readings and tapings are not the same will cassette publication flourish.

BBC radio has been publishing poetry-on-microphone for decades. Poets have been the producers, by and large: Louis MacNeice, W. R. Rogers, and in recent years George MacBeth. BBC producers actually *direct* poets speaking their own poems, as well as actors speaking other people's. In England, poets who read badly on the platform, stiff and shy and monotonous, have been trained for radio, and in the solitude of a studio perform their poems superbly. American poets, oppositely experienced, have opposite talents and failures.

American poets have learned by trial and error to read their poems in public, until the reading has become the most important form of contemporary publication. If American poets can learn to embody the voice alone, the cassette can become a third form of publication.

When you address a microphone, you speak to one person. When you address an auditorium, your eyes scan from side to side. Poets often notice that they read differently to an auditorium full of people, or in a living room to a particular friend or two. Reading for radio is more like reading to one person than it is like reading to a group.

But even more so. The attenuation of senses sharpens the sense of hearing. Every molecule of voice is heard, both intimate and grossly large. Speaking to the microphone requires and enforces an intense concentration, on the reader and eventually on the listener. If the listener isn't rewarded for his intense concentration, he switches off. Old hands at radio often manage this intensity with a manic concentration on the microphone itself—staring at it, crooning to it, the hands gesturing around it in supplication, almost fondling it, the head cocked next to it, praying to this gray object, like some old believer at a rite.

The result can be beautiful. The technology of print brought vision to poetry, the visible line, the pauses of the blank spaces. The dry buzzing space of pause, the fragile sensitivity of the microphone—these realities bring other opportunities.

NATURAL SPEECH

Most major changes in poetic style consider that they return to natural speech. Everybody knows the litany: Dryden after metaphysical conceits, Wordsworth after Neoclassical poetic diction. In this century, Imagism with its "direct description of the thing itself" laid waste to Georgian ornament. Objectivism grows out of Imagism, and embodies the contours of speech. Somewhere among all this, Marianne Moore wanted to write a plain American, that cats and dogs could read.

In the arts as in all things, modernity accelerates change. Every decade or two, new varieties of poetic diction establish themselves, and new revolutions throw them over. In the diversity of American poetry now, there are a number of prevailing poetic dictions—special manners of assembling language, inherited from elders, which involve a distance from common speech. There is still an element of Auden's common-room diction, among a few poets: in a recent volume Daryl Hine re-affirmed "That only the most recherché style, the most affected/Can sustain the weight of time and tears and truth." Such open affectation is rare; other camps are equally mannered without praising mannerism. Minimal objectivism, with its syllables breathed spacially all over the page, seems a distortion of speech—curiously for the sake of speech—like words spoken by people who have trouble moving their lips. And the poetry of fantasy, dream-image poetry, has developed conventions and manners—even a rhetoric—of syntax rather than of diction; it affects conjunctions of the real and fantastic, and mostly achieves only a mechanical derangement.

So one would expect new poets to "return" to natural speech.

Among certain poets, I think we find this return beginning. Diane Wakoski often writes poetry without poetry in it, sentences without metaphor or image, poetry of statement and summary. Louis Simpson's narrative style involves plain talk without metaphor, or nearly without metaphor, telling stories in which the plot does the talking, not flashy language. James Scully's late work is resolutely plain. One thinks of the "plain style" of the sixteenth and seventeenth centuries, the style which C. S. Lewis called "silver." Of course these poets do not write like each other. Nor do I think they are equal in value or in success. Maybe they share only their series of negations: the distrust of fancy talk, of surface, of exhibitionistic language.

This movement toward plain language should not be confused with a middle-aged motion toward "looseness"—or with sloppiness, or with the rhetoric of vulnerability. There is a stylistic equivalent of the banker running off with the chorus girl, while his wife elopes with the gambler. A young poet I talked to recently derided "all those poets who find Whitman at forty, and decide to *get loose*." Uh-huh. Vulnerability *as* rhetoric announces, "I'm going to be sloppy and open, and if you don't like it, you're just another tight-ass, Buddy." On the other hand, the poetry of plain language can be very subtle, very careful; it is first of all careful to *be* plain.

Maybe the plainest is Frank Bidart, who published *Golden State* with Braziller a couple of years ago. The book begins with a sadistic dramatic monologue which I dislike. Then it settles down to autobiographical poems, telling of parents and childhood in language as flat as this:

> The need for the past
>
> is so much at the center of my life
> I write this poem to record my discovery of it,
>
> my reconciliation.

At first I think, who needs language like this?—so abstract, so boring! (The metaphors of "center" and "discovery" are language heightened to the level of Gerald Ford.) Reading it at first, I become angry at this plainness. But I keep on reading.

After a dozen pages, I believe everything he tells me. These autobiographical poems wholly convince me of their serious, inward, intelligent honesty. They are not rhetorically vulnerable. They don't proclaim the thorns or the bleeding. They announce in level tones a judgment which one trusts, because one trusts the man talking.

Then I realize that Bidart is extraordinarily skillful. You don't feel the razor cut you because the razor is so sharp. Every space, every pause, is weighted with the accuracy of a chemist's scale. Though the language looks careless, the poems are intensely careful.

Now "careful" does not mean "good"—any more than "careless" means "bad."

D. H. Lawrence was careless. (Whitman was not careless, whatever they tell you.) And we are tired of careful minimalists with their breathed syllables placed just right—like a picture hanging over a sofa, not a sixteenth of an inch out of place; minor estheticism. And we are tired of "the most recherché style, the most affected," whether it be Audenesque or Surrealistic. But care in the service of expression, care in the service of feeling, is a device of most of the best poetry written, be it by Ben Jonson or by James Wright or by William Bronk.

THE SCHOLAR

A couple of years ago, I wrote an essay about the psychic sources of poetic form. For lack of suitable abstractions, I wound up inventing some characters to embody characteristics of poetic form, which I traced to infantile or autistic origins. *Milktongue* was a love of sound as vowels, like milk in the mouth. *Goatfoot* was the love of sound as dance, like the infant's rhythmic movement. *Twinbird* was the love of resolution, like the two hands which hover at the baby's eyes, identical and opposite. Since these three characters were of course unworded, existing only before language, and without tongues, I had to invent *Priestess*. The Priestess talks dactylic hexameter at Delphi. She gets her material from the three in the forest, and she speaks words to represent this material. She has no idea of what she means by what she says, but she feels "compelled to speak."

This summary exposes what I omitted from that essay. Of course Goatfoot, Milktongue, Twinbird, and the Priestess all inhabit the same poet. The poet can be defined as the innkeeper who entertains all these creatures, and watches them, and makes sure that they don't watch each other.

But there is at least one further character essential to poetic form. He is not one of the psychic *sources*, which is perhaps why I didn't think of him in 1973. But neither is the Priestess. Both of them are links that connect the sources to the written poem.

After the Priestess speaks her dactyls, there is a further process. The Scholar listens, copies down (the Priestess can speak, but she is illiterate), puzzles, scratches his head, wonders if he heard wrong, tries a new word for an old one he might have misheard, returns to the Priestess to listen some more, sighs again, closes his book, cannot sleep, opens it again, puts things together, takes things apart, scratches his head again, decides when to begin and when to end, speaks the words aloud, copies them over—and burns a million candles trying to get the words right.

The Scholar has a beard, many wrinkles, wears a long black gown, and often does not hear his own name when he is spoken to. He is the Rabbi who examines the Talmud. He is the theologian of the middle ages who puzzles for forty years over the meaning of a single pluperfect which may have been spoken by a saint.

Goatfoot and Milktongue come from the first day of birth, Twinbird comes maybe from a week or two later. The Priestess is one-and-a-half years old, maybe two. The Scholar is ten or eleven or even twelve. (That's why I left him out last time. Too old and stodgy.) In racial rather than in personal time, Milktongue and Goatfoot begin as early as mammals begin; Twinbird is a hundred thousand years further along; the Priestess uses sharp stones at the edge of the savannah; the Scholar remembers how the old men conspired to kill an elephant.

And the Scholar is priest, wiseman, seer, rememberer, shaman, bard. He interprets lightening and goats' entrails. He keeps the journal of the tribes' wandering. He carries the book in his head. He goes over and over the texts he received from the scholars before him. After a long time, he makes his decision. He comes out of his tent, out of the monastery, out of the library; he makes his decisions known.

SHAKESPEARE'S LINES IN ACADEMIC DRESS

At last, Shakespeare has been translated into English.

Simon and Schuster has just issued *Macbeth, Hamlet, King Lear,* and *Julius Caesar,* in four separate volumes, with the Shakespearean text on the left-hand side of the page and a modern English paraphrase *en face.* Maurice Charney begins his General Introduction, "The purpose of this series is to make Shakespeare fully intelligible to the modern reader." Thus, on the right-hand page we read, "To be or not to be; that is what really matters." Apparently, "the question" has become unintelligible.

It would be easy to make fun of this endeavor by quoting paraphrases of famous moments—"Tomorrow follows tomorrow, and is followed by tomorrow"—and it would be snobbish. Modern versions of the Bible sound shabby beside the King James, to people who have been nourished on that grandeur. But for centuries egalitarian Christians have recognized that verbal archaism restricts God's word to an elite. There are readers for whom Shakespearean archaism raises an impenetrable wall; for them, an idiomatic trot would be useful, glossing words like "fardel" and "bodkin." When these new texts clarify obsolete language, they do service.

But these editions do more, and they do other. When the general editor compares them to translations—"Ironically, non-English-speaking readers of Shakespeare have always had modernized versions in translation"—I think he misleads us. A good translation into French retains Shakespeare's metaphors, or substitutes equivalent metaphors, and utters itself in rhythms pleasing to the ear. But these modernizations lack music, and frequently remove or explain metaphors. Because they diminish richness more than they explain archaism, these books are pernicious.

Shakespeare's *meaning*—to my ear—resides in the alternate relative volume of his iambic, and in the minute pause after each decasyllable, as much as it resides in his diction, his metaphor, and his images. It does not reside in plot summaries, or in paraphrases: take away sound, take away metaphors and images—and I would as soon use the Classics Comics' *Julius Caesar* as I would Maurice Charney's. Shakespeare is the only Shakespeare there is.

Maybe metaphor, in the minds of the editors, is itself archaic. The General Introduction suggests this notion, when it speaks of Elizabethan "exuberance of expression which is no longer appropriate in modern English," and of "styles of discourse that have gone out of fashion."

To explain a metaphor is to remove it: for "Out, out, brief candle," an editor substitutes "Burn out, burn out, brief candle of life." Another editor explains *while* he removes: when Mark Antony exhorts his listeners, "lend me your ears," the *modernized* phrase is, "listen to me." Or take something merely routine for Shakespeare; the first metaphor in *Hamlet* is simple enough; one watchman challenges another in the darkness: "Stand and *unfold* yourself." What a happy way to ask a man to reveal his identity! Curled defensively behind his shield, the soldier is asked to open up like a butterfly or a flag. But the modern English version contains nothing visual: "Stand still and tell me who you are." Perhaps it is supposed to be modern *because* it has nothing visual in it.

The editors of this series repeatedly warn us that paraphrases are not the real thing, and that "ideally"—the word is used several times—a reader will glance to the right-hand side of the page only when he is baffled. The paraphrase exists only "to clarify," and to make "Shakespeare come alive again." But is "unfold" dead, and "tell me who you are" alive? Is "lend me your ear" dead, and "listen to me" alive?

Really, it is not Shakespeare who is attacked by these paraphrases, but Americans and their language. Are we really incapable of understanding metaphor? Contemporary American poetry is highly metaphorical; so is American popular song, blues, rock music, disc jockey talk, and *Rolling Stone* journalese; so are portions of American speech, notably southern white and northern black.

Not *all* American speech is metaphorical: the speech of corporations, of politicians, and of universities is abstract and boring, without metaphor or image. Compare the language of annual reports with the language of college catalogs, the State of the Union address with the commencement speech; these languages are all the same dead language, which is American Institutional.

The language spoken in the academy is institutional prose, which pursues "meaning" or "understanding" by draining itself of sound and sensuousness, figure and color. English departments typically teach poetry by turning it into bad prose in order to talk about it. In these texts, Shakespeare is translated not into the American idiom but into institutional abstractions, to make him "come alive again."

NOTES ON FOOTNOTES

Yeats's great lines, in "Leda and the Swan," combine Eros and history as no one else ever dreamed of doing:

> A shudder in the loins engenders there
> The broken wall . . .

If we read this poem in *The Norton Anthology of Modern Poetry*, edited by Richard Ellmann and Robert O'Clair, we find that the editors have supplied a footnote, in case we missed the point: "The tragic conclusion of the events caused by Leda's daughters"—they tell us, in their broken-winged prose—"are here foreshadowed by the sexual violence."

Richard Wilbur wrote "As music conjured Ilium from the ground," a line which requires some sophistication in the reading. *But let him require it.* What arrogance to footnote the line, as the editors of another anthology do, "I.e., as Homer evoked Ilium or Troy, in the Iliad." Notice also "evoked," a word picked up from perfume advertisements; we teach our students that "evoked" means something and that "conjured" is mere poetry-talk, which teacher or textbook will clear up for us, telling us what the fumbling poet is "trying to say."

Earlier in the same book, when Eliot speaks of "the unprayable/Prayer at the calamitous annunciation," an unspeakable footnote speculates, "Perhaps meaning that when the annunciation is of calamity—of imminent death—it is no longer possible to pray." *Let me do the speculating, please.*

In *The Norton Anthology of Modern Poetry*, Yeats, always unlucky in his critics, gets the most sordid treatment of anyone. His phrase "Gray Truth" (from "The Song of the Happy Shepherd") is glossed: "Yeats was dismayed, as he indicates in his Autobiography, by the rationalistic, anti-imaginative atmosphere of his time." If he was, I would like to ask what he would think of this dead metaphor, "atmosphere"? The editors footnote "Gray Truth" with prosaic clichés, and appeal from the poet's poem to the outside authority of poet's prose; both actions substantiate the internal argument of all these footnotes: "For prose read *sense* throughout."

Other poets suffer as well. When J. Alfred Prufrock speaks initially of "the room" where "women come and go," the editors footnote presumptuously: "Presumably the room where Prufrock is going to speak to a woman friend."

Get your hand off my sleeve!

When Hart Crane writes, "Invariably when wine redeems the sight," the editors whisper in our ear, "In a state of visionary drunkenness."

Shut up!

But they don't shut up. When Crane says, "Slow/ Applause flows into liquid cynosures," that same boring academic whisper lets me in on the secret; with a conspiratorial leer, it allows, "General wellbeing flows like wine."

It will be objected, doubtless, that I come to the poems with certain advantages not shared by the college sophomores for whom the textbooks are written.

I reject the objection.

In a classroom, the first and longest standing enemies to the teaching of poetry are these notions, common among students, and obviously among many teachers:

1) that poems are *problems* which have *answers*;

2) that there is a *meaning*, which corresponds—in this barbaric esthetic and psychology—to "what the poet was trying to say": some doctrine of intentions accompanied by the poet's riddle-making perversity, or by her incompetence of expression;

3) that there is always, somehow, an answer in the back of the book, or in the teachers' manual, if only somebody will stop being coy and reveal it.

Footnotes like those I have quoted support the back-of-the-book theory, and therefore commit themselves to the war against poetry.

These footnotes deny that the poem is only itself. They indulge in the fallacy of paraphrase: that different expressions can result in emotional and conceptual identity.

These footnotes deny that the poem is multiple—that one can, as with the best sculpture, see different and equally valid poems as one walks around the three dimensions.

They deny that the poem will change from reader to reader, or within the same reader over the years—the way the color of Greek stone changes through the day, hour by hour, according to the sun's height and angle.

These footnotes, *by their existence*, testify that metaphor is aberration—a heresy popular among English teachers—and that prose has validity automatically greater than poetry's.

I accuse "English teachers." I don't mean all of us—but I must mean a majority of us. The authors of the textbooks are English teachers, and they are directly responsible—but I doubt that the author of the great biography of James Joyce, for example, is happy with these footnotes, or that he would have agreed to their presence without pressure from his publisher.

Why does the publisher apply pressure? Because the publisher wishes to sell books, and he knows his audience. He knows his audience of teachers—hostile to the emotional intricacy and precision of metaphor, frightened by the emotional intensity of image—who choose and order the books that students must buy.

THE POET'S PLACE

For some poets, poetry derives from a place. Poem after

poem reaches back and touches this place, and rehearses experiences connected with the place: Wordsworth's "Nature"; the Welsh farms of Dylan Thomas; T. S. Eliot's St. Louis and Dry Salvages; Wallace Stevens's Florida; Walt Whitman and Paumanok; architectural Italy for Ezra Pound; Gloucester for Charles Olson.

Not all poets need or use places. I cannot associate place with William Blake or John Donne. It seems more true that nineteenth- and twentieth-century poets derive their poems from particular places. I suppose you could consider the classic bucolic; you could surely consider the great poetry of T'ang; but I am not thinking only of poetry which is geographic or descriptive. I am thinking of places which to the poets embody or recall a spiritual state.

For some poets place is golden, and the golden place like the golden age is usually unattainable—either because it is in the historical past or because it is in the biographical past of the poet, or both. (Such doubling is a poetic habit.) The poem wishes to attain—perhaps does attain, for a moment—a rare condition of blessedness, which the place sponsors.

I think these places are associated with one experience. (I remember Vernon Watkins telling me, years ago, that all a poet's poems derived from one experience. The statement bewildered me then, and I believe it now.) This experience has been called the "oceanic feeling," when we understand (with a sensation which is often frightening) our connections with everything. There is no demarcation between ourselves and the universe of space or of time. Our smallness among the pieces of time in the universe is terrifying; but our connectedness is comforting.

This experience ties us to the marmoset and to the fern, and to the plankton in the sea. It ties us to

Cleopatra and Ghenghis Khan, and to Ghenghis Khan's horse. I suspect it even ties us to minerals. Reminiscence of the womb gives a shape to the experience, provides it psychically (or even biographically) with a local habitation and a name. This experience becomes the memory of the fulfilled moment when we joined everything and were joined by everything—and we write our poems in the attempt to reach that moment again.

Why should this experience be connected with one place? Usually, I suppose, because we *had* the experience there—beside the waterfall, or in the woods, or by the ocean's breaking wave, or in the hayfields—and had the experience not once but many times. We had it there mostly when we were young—not yet so far from the womb as to forget it, and still able to dream about it; yet old enough to conceptualize and to remember.

What kind of a place must it be? It must be a place where we felt free. It must be a place associated not with school or with conventional endeavor or with competition or with busyness. It must be a place, therefore, in which we can rehearse feelings (and a type of thinking) which belong in evolutionary terms to an earlier condition of humanity. And it is this earlier mind that we wish to stimulate, in poetry. Sometimes we speak as if we wish to return to it; actually, we want it to return to us, and to live with us forever. Therefore the place which is golden is a place where we have loafed and invited the soul, and where the ego—not yet born—has made no demands upon the soul.

One reason this place appears in modern poetry is historical, associated with capitalism, with class structure, and with associated means of travel. For the past two hundred years, in the industrial and mechanical centuries, most poets have grown up in city or in town.

City or town for the middle classes has been the place of work; for a child, it has been the place of school. The country and the seashore have been the places of freedom and laziness—be it for Dylan Thomas on his families' (not his schoolteacher father's) farm or T. S. Eliot at the summer shore or Charles Olson at the vacation place of Gloucester, away from the post office (and the school) of Worcester, or Ezra Pound traveling through Italy in summer with his great aunt. Old relatives make fewer demands upon us than parents do; we are *spoiled* by our grandparents, we relax on the receptive bosom which makes no demands upon us. (For "being spoiled," read "regressing" throughout!) Or we merely live in a resort hotel without washing the dishes, and we walk by the ocean where the waves sing to us songs about death, and salt hay rubs against salt hay, and our soul hovers over us tentatively free of the body and its daily concerns.

For Wallace Stevens, that Puritan in love with opulence, the flamingos and oranges of Florida were the sources of poems—the dream made flesh in middle life. Not by coincidence, he visited this dream landscape on holiday from the insurance business, away from the thin men of Haddam and Hartford.

I think of Whitman and "Out of the Cradle." The secret place is often the mother, I suppose, the womb which was our original place of connectedness; therefore, in its connectedness, the womb-experience becomes the introduction to death—mother death, the place we will enter to dissolve the personality and the ego we have accrued in the years since the womb; when we re-enter the molecular universe.

The real geography is accidental, and Eliot's Gloucester has little to do with Olson's. In the psyche the poetic place, however, is always the same place—mother and grave and being.